Guac Your 100 Recipes for Avocado Lovers

Sweet Tooth Bakery

Copyright © 2023 Sweet Tooth Bakery
All rights reserved.

Contents

INTRODUCTION 7
1. Avocado Toast with Poached Egg 8
2. Guacamole with Tortilla Chips 9
3. Avocado and Tomato Salad 10
4. Avocado Stuffed with Quinoa Salad 11
5. Avocado Smoothie with Spinach and Banana 12
6. Avocado Caprese Salad 13
7. Grilled Chicken and Avocado Wraps 14
8. Avocado and Shrimp Ceviche 16
9. Avocado and Black Bean Quesadillas 17
10. Avocado Tuna Salad 18
11. Avocado and Cucumber Sushi Rolls 19
12. Avocado and Bacon Grilled Cheese Sandwich 20
13. Avocado and Corn Salad 21
14. Avocado and Chickpea Salad 22
15. Avocado and Smoked Salmon Benedict 23
16. Avocado and Mango Salsa 24
17. Avocado and Goat Cheese Stuffed Chicken Breast 25
18. Avocado and Cilantro Lime Rice Bowl 27
19. Avocado and Tomato Bruschetta 28
20. Avocado and Turkey Club Sandwich 29
21. Avocado and Lime Ice Cream 30
22. Avocado and Bacon Deviled Eggs 31
23. Avocado and Pesto Pasta 32
24. Avocado and Roasted Red Pepper Hummus Wrap 33
25. Avocado and Black Bean Burritos 34
26. Avocado and Shrimp Salad 36
27. Avocado and Sweet Potato Hash 36

28. Avocado and Grilled Vegetable Panini 38
29. Avocado and Tomato Gazpacho 39
30. Avocado and Feta Stuffed Portobello Mushrooms 40
31. Avocado and Chicken Caesar Salad 41
32. Avocado and Strawberry Smoothie 43
33. Avocado and Spinach Stuffed Chicken Breast 43
34. Avocado and Quinoa Stuffed Bell Peppers 44
35. Avocado and Bacon Pasta Salad 46
36. Avocado and Tofu Stir-Fry 47
37. Avocado and Corn Chowder 48
38. Avocado and Goat Cheese Crostini 49
39. Avocado and Tomato Omelette 50
40. Avocado and Black Bean Salsa 51
41. Avocado and Basil Pesto Pizza 52
42. Avocado and Smoked Salmon Salad 53
43. Avocado and Cucumber Soup 54
44. Avocado and Chicken Lettuce Wraps 55
45. Avocado and Lime Pound Cake 56
46. Avocado and Bacon Breakfast Burrito 57
47. Avocado and Chickpea Stuffed Bell Peppers 59
48. Avocado and Shrimp Pasta 60
49. Avocado and Tomato Quinoa Bowl 61
50. Avocado and Goat Cheese Stuffed Mushrooms 62
51. Avocado and Cilantro Lime Dressing 63
52. Avocado and Bacon Wrapped Shrimp 64
53. Avocado and Black Bean Enchiladas 65
54. Avocado and Tomato Grilled Cheese Sandwich 67
55. Avocado and Mango Smoothie 68
56. Avocado and Spinach Stuffed Mushrooms 69

57. Avocado and Quinoa Salad 70
58. Avocado and Bacon Egg Cups 72
59. Avocado and Chicken Tortilla Soup 73
60. Avocado and Lime Cheesecake 74
61. Avocado and Tomato Pita Sandwich 75
62. Avocado and Cucumber Salad 76
63. Avocado and Bacon Potato Salad 77
64. Avocado and Chicken Fajitas 78
65. Avocado and Spinach Quiche 79
66. Avocado and Grilled Shrimp Skewers 81
67. Avocado and Tomato Crostini 82
68. Avocado and Corn Quesadillas 83
69. Avocado and Goat Cheese Stuffed Burger 84
70. Avocado and Lime Mousse 85
71. Avocado and Bacon Stuffed Mushrooms 86
72. Avocado and Black Bean Tacos 88
73. Avocado and Tomato Frittata 89
74. Avocado and Mango Salad 90
75. Avocado and Spinach Smoothie 91
76. Avocado and Quinoa Stuffed Zucchini 92
77. Avocado and Bacon Stuffed Jalapenos 93
78. Avocado and Chicken Salad Wrap 94
79. Avocado and Lime Tart 95
80. Avocado and Tomato Pasta 96
81. Avocado and Cucumber Roll-Ups 98
82. Avocado and Black Bean Burgers 99
83. Avocado and Goat Cheese Stuffed Peppers 100
84. Avocado and Lime Sorbet 101
85. Avocado and Bacon Mac and Cheese 103

86. Avocado and Chicken Lettuce Cups 104
87. Avocado and Strawberry Salad 105
88. Avocado and Spinach Pesto Pasta 106
89. Avocado and Quinoa Stuffed Tomatoes 107
90. Avocado and Bacon Tacos 109
91. Avocado and Tomato Salsa 110
92. Avocado and Corn Fritters 111
93. Avocado and Goat Cheese Stuffed Chicken 112
94. Avocado and Lime Popsicles 114
95. Avocado and Tomato Tartines 115
96. Avocado and Black Bean Stuffed Sweet Potatoes 116
97. Avocado and Cucumber Gazpacho 117
98. Avocado and Bacon Breakfast Pizza 118
99. Avocado and Chicken Fajita Salad 119
100. Avocado and Lime Margarita 121
CONCLUSION 123

INTRODUCTION

Welcome to Guac Your World: 100 Recipes for Avocado Lovers! If you're an avocado lover, this cookbook is the perfect resource for you. Here, we've collected an abundance of recipes featuring the amazing avocado, a creamy, delicious, and nutritious fruit.

Avocados are a special type of fruit, offering a wide range of essential minerals and vitamins. They are known for their high content of healthy fats and antioxidants that can help protect against certain types of chronic diseases. In addition, they are also rich in fiber, which can help promote a healthy digestive system.

The recipes in this cookbook cover a wide gamut of dishes, from breakfast to dinner, from appetizers to desserts. There are savory meals, including sandwiches, burritos, and quesadillas, as well as sweet creations, such as smoothies and ice creams. All of the recipes incorporate avocado in some way, and all are easy to make. Whether you're searching for a quick snack or a complex dinner, this book has something for everyone.

In addition to the recipes, this cookbook contains an introduction to the versatility of avocado, as well as a listing of its various benefits. You'll also find cooking tips and suggestions for substitutions and variations.

We hope you enjoy exploring all the delicious possibilities encompassed in this cookbook. From creamy avocado salads to indulgent desserts, your dinner table will be reinvented with this book in hand. Prepare to guac your world!

1. Avocado Toast with Poached Egg

Avocado Toast with Poached Egg is a delicious and nutritious breakfast or brunch option that is packed with healthy fats, protein, and fiber. The creamy avocado spread on a crispy toast, topped with a perfectly poached egg, makes for a satisfying and flavorful meal to start your day.
Serving: 1 Serving: Preparation time: 10 minutes
Ready time: 15 minutes

Ingredients:
- 1 ripe avocado
- 1 tablespoon lemon juice
- Salt and pepper to taste
- 2 slices of whole grain bread
- 2 large eggs
- 1 teaspoon white vinegar (optional)
- Red pepper flakes (optional, for garnish)
- Fresh cilantro or parsley (optional, for garnish)

Instructions:
1. In a small bowl, mash the ripe avocado with a fork until smooth. Add lemon juice, salt, and pepper to taste. Mix well and set aside.
2. Toast the slices of whole grain bread until golden and crispy.
3. While the bread is toasting, fill a medium-sized saucepan with water and bring it to a gentle simmer. Add the white vinegar (optional) to the water, which helps the eggs hold their shape during poaching.
4. Crack one egg into a small bowl or ramekin. Create a gentle whirlpool in the simmering water by stirring it with a spoon. Carefully slide the egg into the center of the whirlpool. Repeat with the second egg.
5. Allow the eggs to poach for about 3-4 minutes for a soft, runny yolk or 5-6 minutes for a firmer yolk.
6. While the eggs are poaching, spread the mashed avocado evenly onto the toasted bread slices.
7. Using a slotted spoon, carefully remove the poached eggs from the water and place them on top of the avocado spread.
8. Sprinkle with red pepper flakes and fresh cilantro or parsley, if desired.
9. Serve immediately and enjoy!

Nutrition information per Serving: - Calories: 380
- Fat: 22g
- Carbohydrates: 32g
- Fiber: 12g
- Protein: 18g

2. Guacamole with Tortilla Chips

Guacamole with Tortilla Chips is a classic Mexican dish that is loved by many for its creamy and flavorful taste. This delicious appetizer is perfect for parties, game nights, or simply as a snack. Made with ripe avocados, fresh vegetables, and a hint of lime juice, this guacamole is sure to be a crowd-pleaser. Serve it with crispy tortilla chips for a satisfying and addictive combination.

Serving: 4 servings
Preparation time: 15 minutes
Ready time: 15 minutes

Ingredients:
- 3 ripe avocados
- 1 small red onion, finely diced
- 1 jalapeno pepper, seeds removed and finely diced
- 2 tomatoes, seeds removed and diced
- 1/4 cup fresh cilantro, chopped
- 2 cloves of garlic, minced
- Juice of 1 lime
- Salt and pepper to taste
- Tortilla chips, for Serving:

Instructions:
1. Cut the avocados in half, remove the pits, and scoop the flesh into a bowl. Mash the avocados with a fork until smooth but still slightly chunky.
2. Add the diced red onion, jalapeno pepper, tomatoes, cilantro, and minced garlic to the bowl with the mashed avocados.
3. Squeeze the juice of one lime over the mixture and season with salt and pepper to taste. Stir well to combine all the Ingredients.

4. Taste and adjust the seasoning if needed. If you prefer a spicier guacamole, you can add more diced jalapeno pepper.
5. Transfer the guacamole to a serving bowl and garnish with a sprig of cilantro if desired.
6. Serve the guacamole with tortilla chips on the side for dipping.

Nutrition information per Serving: - Calories: 180
- Fat: 15g
- Carbohydrates: 12g
- Fiber: 8g
- Protein: 3g

Note: Nutrition information may vary depending on the brand of tortilla chips used.

3. Avocado and Tomato Salad

Avocado and Tomato Salad is a refreshing and nutritious dish that combines the creamy texture of avocados with the juicy sweetness of tomatoes. This salad is not only delicious but also packed with essential vitamins and minerals. It is a perfect side dish for any meal or can be enjoyed on its own as a light and healthy lunch option.

Serving: 4 servings
Preparation time: 10 minutes
Ready time: 10 minutes

Ingredients:
- 2 ripe avocados
- 2 large tomatoes
- 1 small red onion
- 1/4 cup fresh cilantro, chopped
- 2 tablespoons extra virgin olive oil
- 1 tablespoon fresh lemon juice
- Salt and pepper to taste

Instructions:
1. Start by slicing the avocados in half, removing the pit, and scooping out the flesh. Cut the avocado into bite-sized chunks and place them in a large mixing bowl.

2. Next, dice the tomatoes into small pieces and add them to the bowl with the avocados.
3. Finely chop the red onion and cilantro, and add them to the bowl as well.
4. In a separate small bowl, whisk together the olive oil, lemon juice, salt, and pepper to make the dressing.
5. Pour the dressing over the avocado and tomato mixture and gently toss everything together until well combined.
6. Taste and adjust the seasoning if needed.
7. Let the salad sit for a few minutes to allow the flavors to meld together.
8. Serve the avocado and tomato salad chilled or at room temperature.

Nutrition information per Serving: - Calories: 180
- Fat: 14g
- Carbohydrates: 12g
- Fiber: 7g
- Protein: 2g
- Vitamin C: 20% of the daily recommended intake
- Vitamin K: 26% of the daily recommended intake
- Potassium: 480mg

4. Avocado Stuffed with Quinoa Salad

Avocado Stuffed with Quinoa Salad is a delicious and nutritious dish that combines the creaminess of avocado with the protein-packed goodness of quinoa. This recipe is perfect for a light lunch or as a side dish for dinner. The combination of flavors and textures will leave you satisfied and wanting more!
Serving: 2 servings
Preparation time: 15 minutes
Ready time: 20 minutes

Ingredients:
- 2 ripe avocados
- 1 cup cooked quinoa
- 1/2 cup cherry tomatoes, halved
- 1/4 cup red onion, finely chopped

- 1/4 cup cucumber, diced
- 1/4 cup fresh cilantro, chopped
- 1 tablespoon lime juice
- 1 tablespoon olive oil
- Salt and pepper to taste

Instructions:
1. Cut the avocados in half lengthwise and remove the pits. Scoop out a little bit of the flesh from each avocado half to create a larger cavity for the quinoa salad. Set aside.
2. In a medium-sized bowl, combine the cooked quinoa, cherry tomatoes, red onion, cucumber, and cilantro. Mix well.
3. In a small bowl, whisk together the lime juice, olive oil, salt, and pepper. Pour the dressing over the quinoa salad and toss until everything is well coated.
4. Spoon the quinoa salad into the hollowed-out avocados, dividing it evenly among them.
5. Serve immediately and enjoy!

Nutrition information:
- Calories: 320
- Fat: 20g
- Carbohydrates: 30g
- Fiber: 12g
- Protein: 8g

Note: Nutrition information may vary depending on the size of the avocados and the specific brands of Ingredients used.

5. Avocado Smoothie with Spinach and Banana

This Avocado Smoothie with Spinach and Banana is a delicious and nutritious way to start your day. Packed with vitamins, minerals, and fiber, this smoothie will give you the energy you need to tackle your day. The combination of creamy avocado, nutrient-rich spinach, and sweet banana creates a perfectly balanced and refreshing drink. Give it a try and enjoy the benefits of this green powerhouse!
Serving: 2 servings
Preparation time: 5 minutes

Ready time: 5 minutes

Ingredients:
- 1 ripe avocado, pitted and peeled
- 1 ripe banana
- 1 cup fresh spinach leaves
- 1 cup almond milk (or any other milk of your choice)
- 1 tablespoon honey or maple syrup (optional, for added sweetness)
- Ice cubes (optional, for a chilled smoothie)

Instructions:
1. In a blender, combine the avocado, banana, spinach, almond milk, and sweetener (if using).
2. Blend on high speed until all the Ingredients are well combined and smooth.
3. If desired, add a few ice cubes and blend again until the smoothie is chilled.
4. Pour the smoothie into glasses and serve immediately.

Nutrition information per Serving: - Calories: 220
- Fat: 12g
- Carbohydrates: 28g
- Fiber: 8g
- Protein: 4g
- Vitamin A: 40% of the Daily Value
- Vitamin C: 30% of the Daily Value
- Calcium: 20% of the Daily Value
- Iron: 10% of the Daily Value

Note: Nutrition information may vary depending on the specific Ingredients and brands used.

6. Avocado Caprese Salad

Avocado Caprese Salad is a refreshing and vibrant dish that combines the creaminess of avocado with the classic flavors of a Caprese salad. This salad is perfect for a light lunch or as a side dish for a summer barbecue. With its colorful presentation and delicious taste, it is sure to be a hit at any gathering.

Serving: 4 servings
Preparation time: 15 minutes
Ready time: 15 minutes

Ingredients:
- 2 ripe avocados, sliced
- 2 large tomatoes, sliced
- 8 ounces fresh mozzarella cheese, sliced
- 1/4 cup fresh basil leaves
- 2 tablespoons extra virgin olive oil
- 2 tablespoons balsamic glaze
- Salt and pepper to taste

Instructions:
1. Arrange the avocado slices, tomato slices, and mozzarella cheese slices on a serving platter, alternating them in a circular pattern.
2. Tuck the fresh basil leaves in between the avocado, tomato, and mozzarella slices.
3. Drizzle the extra virgin olive oil and balsamic glaze over the salad.
4. Season with salt and pepper to taste.
5. Serve immediately and enjoy!

Nutrition information per Serving: - Calories: 250
- Fat: 20g
- Carbohydrates: 10g
- Protein: 10g
- Fiber: 6g
- Sugar: 3g
- Sodium: 200mg

Note: Nutrition information may vary depending on the specific Ingredients and brands used.

7. Grilled Chicken and Avocado Wraps

Grilled Chicken and Avocado Wraps are a delicious and healthy option for a quick and satisfying meal. Packed with protein from the grilled chicken and healthy fats from the avocado, these wraps are perfect for lunch or dinner. The combination of flavors and textures will leave you wanting more!

Serving: 4 wraps
Preparation time: 15 minutes
Ready time: 30 minutes

Ingredients:
- 2 boneless, skinless chicken breasts
- 1 tablespoon olive oil
- 1 teaspoon paprika
- 1 teaspoon garlic powder
- Salt and pepper to taste
- 4 large whole wheat tortillas
- 1 ripe avocado, sliced
- 1 cup shredded lettuce
- 1/2 cup diced tomatoes
- 1/4 cup diced red onion
- 1/4 cup chopped fresh cilantro
- 1/4 cup Greek yogurt or sour cream (optional)

Instructions:
1. Preheat your grill or grill pan over medium-high heat.
2. In a small bowl, mix together the olive oil, paprika, garlic powder, salt, and pepper to create a marinade for the chicken.
3. Place the chicken breasts in a resealable plastic bag and pour the marinade over them. Seal the bag and massage the marinade into the chicken, ensuring it is evenly coated. Let it marinate for at least 15 minutes.
4. Grill the chicken breasts for about 6-8 minutes per side, or until they reach an internal temperature of 165°F (74°C). Remove from the grill and let them rest for a few minutes before slicing.
5. Warm the tortillas on the grill for about 30 seconds on each side, or until they are pliable.
6. To assemble the wraps, place a few slices of grilled chicken on each tortilla. Top with avocado slices, shredded lettuce, diced tomatoes, red onion, and chopped cilantro. Add a dollop of Greek yogurt or sour cream if desired.
7. Fold in the sides of the tortilla and roll it up tightly, securing it with a toothpick if necessary.
8. Serve the Grilled Chicken and Avocado Wraps immediately and enjoy!

Nutrition information per Serving: - Calories: 350
- Fat: 12g
- Carbohydrates: 32g
- Protein: 28g
- Fiber: 8g

8. Avocado and Shrimp Ceviche

Avocado and Shrimp Ceviche is a refreshing and flavorful dish that combines the creaminess of avocado with the tanginess of lime and the succulent taste of shrimp. This dish is perfect for a light lunch or as an appetizer for a summer gathering. The combination of fresh Ingredients makes it a healthy and delicious choice.

Serving: 4 servings
Preparation time: 20 minutes
Ready time: 30 minutes

Ingredients:
- 1 pound of cooked shrimp, peeled and deveined
- 2 ripe avocados, diced
- 1 red onion, finely chopped
- 1 jalapeno pepper, seeded and minced
- 1 cup of cherry tomatoes, halved
- 1/2 cup of fresh cilantro, chopped
- Juice of 3 limes
- Salt and pepper to taste

Instructions:
1. In a large bowl, combine the cooked shrimp, diced avocados, chopped red onion, minced jalapeno pepper, halved cherry tomatoes, and chopped cilantro.
2. Squeeze the juice of 3 limes over the mixture and season with salt and pepper to taste.
3. Gently toss all the Ingredients together until well combined.
4. Cover the bowl with plastic wrap and refrigerate for at least 10 minutes to allow the flavors to meld together.

5. Serve the avocado and shrimp ceviche chilled, either on its own or with tortilla chips or crackers.

Nutrition information per Serving: - Calories: 250
- Fat: 12g
- Carbohydrates: 12g
- Protein: 25g
- Fiber: 6g
- Sugar: 2g
- Sodium: 300mg

Note: Nutrition information may vary depending on the specific Ingredients and brands used.

9. Avocado and Black Bean Quesadillas

Avocado and Black Bean Quesadillas are a delicious and nutritious twist on the classic Mexican dish. Packed with protein, fiber, and healthy fats, these quesadillas are not only satisfying but also incredibly flavorful. The combination of creamy avocado, hearty black beans, and melted cheese makes for a mouthwatering filling that will leave you wanting more. Whether you're looking for a quick and easy lunch or a crowd-pleasing appetizer, these quesadillas are sure to be a hit!
Serving: 4 quesadillas
Preparation time: 10 minutes
Ready time: 20 minutes

Ingredients:
- 4 large flour tortillas
- 1 ripe avocado, sliced
- 1 cup canned black beans, rinsed and drained
- 1 cup shredded cheddar cheese
- 1/2 cup diced red onion
- 1/4 cup chopped fresh cilantro
- 1 teaspoon ground cumin
- 1/2 teaspoon chili powder
- Salt and pepper to taste
- Cooking spray or olive oil for greasing

Instructions:
1. Preheat a large skillet or griddle over medium heat.
2. In a small bowl, mash the black beans with a fork until they form a chunky paste.
3. In another small bowl, combine the diced red onion, chopped cilantro, ground cumin, chili powder, salt, and pepper. Mix well.
4. Lay one flour tortilla flat on a clean surface. Spread a quarter of the mashed black beans evenly over half of the tortilla.
5. Layer sliced avocado on top of the black beans, followed by a quarter of the onion and cilantro mixture.
6. Sprinkle a quarter of the shredded cheddar cheese over the top.
7. Fold the tortilla in half, pressing down gently to seal the filling inside.
8. Repeat steps 4-7 with the remaining tortillas and filling Ingredients.
9. Lightly grease the preheated skillet or griddle with cooking spray or olive oil.
10. Place the quesadillas on the skillet or griddle and cook for 2-3 minutes on each side, or until the tortillas are golden brown and the cheese is melted.
11. Remove the quesadillas from the heat and let them cool for a minute before slicing into wedges.
12. Serve the avocado and black bean quesadillas warm with your favorite salsa, guacamole, or sour cream.

Nutrition information per Serving: - Calories: 350
- Fat: 15g
- Carbohydrates: 40g
- Fiber: 10g
- Protein: 15g
- Sodium: 400mg

Note: Nutrition information may vary depending on the brand and quantity of Ingredients used.

10. Avocado Tuna Salad

Avocado Tuna Salad is a delicious and healthy lunch that takes only 10 minutes to make. It combines the hearty protein from tuna with the creamy goodness of the avocado, and the zing of garlic and lemon to bring this salad to life.

Serving: 2
Preparation Time: 5 minutes
Ready Time: 10 minutes

Ingredients:
- 2 cans of tuna
- 2 avocados, diced
- 2 cloves of garlic, minced
- Juice from 1/2 lemon
- 2 tablespoons of olive oil
- Salt and pepper to taste

Instructions:
1. Drain the tuna and discard the cans.
2. In a bowl, add the tuna, avocados, garlic and olive oil.
3. Squeeze in the lemon juice and add the pepper and salt to the mix.
4. Gently stir all of the Ingredients together until blended.
5. Serve and enjoy!

Nutrition information: Per Serving - Calories: 385, Fat: 26.4g, Cholesterol: 50mg, Sodium: 414mg, Carbohydrates: 11.3g, Protein: 25.6g

11. Avocado and Cucumber Sushi Rolls

Avocado and Cucumber Sushi Rolls is a quick and easy Japanese-style dinner or snack. This vegan-friendly sushi uses seaweed, rice, avocado and cucumber, and is a great way to get your healthy sushi fix.
Serving: 4
Preparation time: 15 minutes
Ready time: 15 minutes

Ingredients:
- 4 sheets nori seaweed
- 2 cups cooked white sushi rice
- 1 cucumber, peeled and cut into matchsticks
- 1 avocado, thinly sliced

Instructions:
1. Place a sheet of nori on a sushi rolling mat. Spread 2/3 cup of cooked sushi rice onto the nori, leaving a ½ inch of space on the top and bottom of the nori.
2. Arrange 4-5 slices of avocado and 4-5 cucumber slices onto the rice.
3. With dry hands, roll the sushi by lifting the closest edge of the mat and pressing it away from you. Gently press the sushi roll as you roll to shape and secure it.
4. Cut the sushi roll into 4 pieces using a sharp knife.

Nutrition information:
Per serving: Calories 288; Total Fat 7g (Saturated 1g) ; Cholesterol 0mg; Sodium 236mg; Carbohydrate 46g (Dietary Fiber 4g) ; Protein 5g

12. Avocado and Bacon Grilled Cheese Sandwich

Avocado and Bacon Grilled Cheese Sandwich is a delicious twist on the classic grilled cheese sandwich. The creamy avocado and crispy bacon add a burst of flavor to this comforting and satisfying meal. It's perfect for a quick lunch or dinner option that will leave you wanting more.
Serving: 2 sandwiches
Preparation time: 10 minutes
Ready time: 20 minutes

Ingredients:
- 4 slices of bread (your choice of bread)
- 1 ripe avocado, sliced
- 4 slices of bacon, cooked until crispy
- 4 slices of cheddar cheese
- 2 tablespoons of butter, softened

Instructions:
1. Preheat a skillet or griddle over medium heat.
2. Lay out the four slices of bread and spread butter on one side of each slice.
3. Place two slices of bread, buttered side down, on the skillet or griddle.
4. Layer each slice of bread with a slice of cheddar cheese, followed by avocado slices and crispy bacon.

5. Top each sandwich with another slice of cheddar cheese and place the remaining slices of bread on top, buttered side up.
6. Cook the sandwiches for about 3-4 minutes on each side, or until the bread is golden brown and the cheese has melted.
7. Remove the sandwiches from the skillet or griddle and let them cool for a minute before slicing them in half.
8. Serve the Avocado and Bacon Grilled Cheese Sandwiches warm and enjoy!

Nutrition information per Serving: - Calories: 480
- Fat: 32g
- Carbohydrates: 30g
- Protein: 20g
- Fiber: 6g

13. Avocado and Corn Salad

This light and summery Avocado and Corn Salad is a delicious and easy-to-make side dish that goes perfectly with any meal. It's packed with flavorful avocado, juicy corn kernels, and vibrant herbs.
Serving: 6
Preparation time: 15 minutes
Ready time: 15 minutes

Ingredients:
-2 avocados, diced
-1 1/2 cups cooked corn kernels
-1/4 cup olive oil
-2 tablespoons lime juice
-2 tablespoons chopped fresh cilantro
-1 tablespoon chopped fresh chives
-1/2 teaspoon salt
-Ground black pepper

Instructions:
1. In a large bowl, combine the diced avocado, corn kernels, olive oil, lime juice, cilantro, chives, salt, and pepper.

2. Gently toss the Ingredients together until everything is coated with the dressing.
3. Taste and adjust seasoning as desired.
4. Serve immediately, or store in the fridge for up to 24 hours.

Nutrition information: per serving -calories 209, fat 17 g, saturated fat 2.5 g, carbohydrates 13.7 g, fiber 4.5 g, sugar 1.6 g, protein 3.2 g, sodium 120 mg

14. Avocado and Chickpea Salad

Avocado and Chickpea Salad is a refreshing and nutritious dish that combines the creaminess of avocado with the protein-packed goodness of chickpeas. This salad is not only delicious but also incredibly easy to make, making it a perfect option for a quick and healthy meal.
Serving: 2 servings
Preparation time: 10 minutes
Ready time: 10 minutes

Ingredients:
- 1 ripe avocado, diced
- 1 cup cooked chickpeas
- 1 small red onion, finely chopped
- 1 small cucumber, diced
- 1 small tomato, diced
- 1/4 cup fresh cilantro, chopped
- Juice of 1 lemon
- 2 tablespoons olive oil
- Salt and pepper to taste

Instructions:
1. In a large bowl, combine the diced avocado, cooked chickpeas, red onion, cucumber, tomato, and cilantro.
2. In a small bowl, whisk together the lemon juice, olive oil, salt, and pepper.
3. Pour the dressing over the avocado and chickpea mixture and gently toss until well combined.
4. Taste and adjust the seasoning if needed.

5. Serve the salad immediately or refrigerate for a few hours to allow the flavors to meld together.

Nutrition information per Serving: - Calories: 250
- Fat: 15g
- Carbohydrates: 25g
- Fiber: 10g
- Protein: 8g
- Sugar: 4g
- Sodium: 200mg

Note: Nutrition information may vary depending on the specific Ingredients and brands used.

15. Avocado and Smoked Salmon Benedict

Avocado and Smoked Salmon Benedict is a delicious and nutritious twist on the classic Eggs Benedict. This dish combines the creaminess of avocado, the smoky flavor of salmon, and the richness of poached eggs, all topped with a tangy hollandaise sauce. It's the perfect brunch option for avocado and salmon lovers!

Serving: 2 servings
Preparation time: 15 minutes
Ready time: 25 minutes

Ingredients:
- 2 English muffins, split and toasted
- 1 ripe avocado, sliced
- 4 slices of smoked salmon
- 4 large eggs
- 1 tablespoon white vinegar
- Fresh dill, for garnish

For the hollandaise sauce:
- 3 large egg yolks
- 1 tablespoon lemon juice
- 1/2 cup unsalted butter, melted
- Salt and pepper to taste

Instructions:

1. To make the hollandaise sauce, fill a saucepan with a few inches of water and bring it to a simmer over medium heat. In a heatproof bowl, whisk together the egg yolks and lemon juice until well combined.
2. Place the bowl over the simmering water, making sure the bottom of the bowl doesn't touch the water. Continue whisking the egg yolk mixture while slowly pouring in the melted butter. Whisk until the sauce thickens, about 3-4 minutes. Season with salt and pepper. Remove from heat and set aside.
3. Fill a large saucepan with water and bring it to a gentle simmer. Add the white vinegar to the water.
4. Crack one egg into a small bowl. Using a spoon, create a gentle whirlpool in the simmering water and carefully slide the egg into the center of the whirlpool. Repeat with the remaining eggs. Poach the eggs for about 3-4 minutes or until the whites are set but the yolks are still runny. Remove the eggs with a slotted spoon and drain on a paper towel.
5. To assemble the Benedict, place the toasted English muffin halves on a plate. Top each half with sliced avocado and a slice of smoked salmon.
6. Carefully place a poached egg on top of each salmon slice. Spoon the hollandaise sauce generously over the eggs.
7. Garnish with fresh dill and season with salt and pepper if desired.
8. Serve immediately and enjoy!

Nutrition information per Serving: - Calories: 450
- Fat: 32g
- Carbohydrates: 25g
- Protein: 18g
- Fiber: 6g

16. Avocado and Mango Salsa

Avocado and Mango Salsa is a refreshing and vibrant dish that combines the creaminess of avocado with the sweetness of mango. This salsa is perfect as a dip, topping for grilled meats or fish, or even as a side dish. With its bright colors and delicious flavors, it is sure to be a hit at any gathering or meal.
Serving: 4 servings
Preparation time: 15 minutes
Ready time: 15 minutes

Ingredients:
- 1 ripe avocado, diced
- 1 ripe mango, diced
- 1/2 red onion, finely chopped
- 1 jalapeno pepper, seeds removed and finely chopped
- 1/4 cup fresh cilantro, chopped
- Juice of 1 lime
- Salt and pepper to taste

Instructions:
1. In a medium-sized bowl, combine the diced avocado, mango, red onion, jalapeno pepper, and cilantro.
2. Squeeze the juice of one lime over the mixture and gently toss to combine.
3. Season with salt and pepper to taste.
4. Serve immediately or refrigerate for up to 1 hour to allow the flavors to meld together.
5. Enjoy as a dip with tortilla chips, as a topping for grilled meats or fish, or as a side dish.

Nutrition information per Serving: - Calories: 120
- Fat: 7g
- Carbohydrates: 15g
- Fiber: 5g
- Protein: 2g
- Vitamin C: 45% of the daily recommended intake
- Vitamin A: 20% of the daily recommended intake

17. Avocado and Goat Cheese Stuffed Chicken Breast

Avocado and Goat Cheese Stuffed Chicken Breast is a delicious and healthy dish that combines the creaminess of avocado and the tanginess of goat cheese. This recipe is perfect for a special dinner or a weeknight meal that will impress your family and friends. The chicken breast is stuffed with a flavorful mixture of avocado and goat cheese, then baked to perfection. It's a dish that is sure to become a favorite!

Serving: 4 servings
Preparation time: 15 minutes
Ready time: 35 minutes

Ingredients:
- 4 boneless, skinless chicken breasts
- 1 ripe avocado, pitted and mashed
- 4 ounces goat cheese, crumbled
- 2 tablespoons fresh cilantro, chopped
- 1 teaspoon garlic powder
- 1 teaspoon onion powder
- 1/2 teaspoon salt
- 1/4 teaspoon black pepper
- 1 tablespoon olive oil

Instructions:
1. Preheat your oven to 375°F (190°C).
2. In a bowl, combine the mashed avocado, goat cheese, cilantro, garlic powder, onion powder, salt, and black pepper. Mix well until all the Ingredients are evenly incorporated.
3. Using a sharp knife, make a horizontal slit in each chicken breast to create a pocket for the stuffing. Be careful not to cut all the way through.
4. Stuff each chicken breast with the avocado and goat cheese mixture, dividing it equally among the four breasts.
5. Heat the olive oil in a large oven-safe skillet over medium-high heat. Once hot, add the stuffed chicken breasts to the skillet and sear them for about 2 minutes on each side, or until they are golden brown.
6. Transfer the skillet to the preheated oven and bake for 20-25 minutes, or until the chicken is cooked through and no longer pink in the center.
7. Remove the skillet from the oven and let the chicken rest for a few minutes before serving.
8. Serve the Avocado and Goat Cheese Stuffed Chicken Breast with your favorite side dishes, such as roasted vegetables or a fresh salad.

Nutrition information per Serving: - Calories: 320
- Fat: 18g
- Carbohydrates: 4g
- Protein: 35g
- Fiber: 2g

18. Avocado and Cilantro Lime Rice Bowl

This Avocado and Cilantro Lime Rice Bowl is a refreshing and nutritious meal that combines the creaminess of avocado with the zesty flavors of cilantro and lime. Packed with healthy fats, fiber, and vitamins, this dish is not only delicious but also good for you. Whether you're looking for a quick lunch or a light dinner, this recipe is sure to satisfy your taste buds and keep you feeling satisfied.

Serving: 2 servings
Preparation time: 10 minutes
Ready time: 20 minutes

Ingredients:
- 1 cup cooked brown rice
- 1 ripe avocado, sliced
- 1/4 cup fresh cilantro, chopped
- 1 lime, juiced
- 1 tablespoon olive oil
- 1/2 teaspoon salt
- 1/4 teaspoon black pepper
- Optional toppings: diced tomatoes, sliced red onion, corn kernels

Instructions:
1. In a medium bowl, combine the cooked brown rice, chopped cilantro, lime juice, olive oil, salt, and black pepper. Mix well to ensure the flavors are evenly distributed.
2. Divide the rice mixture into two bowls.
3. Top each bowl with sliced avocado and any optional toppings you desire, such as diced tomatoes, sliced red onion, or corn kernels.
4. Serve immediately and enjoy!

Nutrition information:
- Calories: 320
- Fat: 18g
- Carbohydrates: 36g
- Fiber: 9g
- Protein: 6g
- Vitamin C: 20% of the daily recommended intake

- Iron: 10% of the daily recommended intake

19. Avocado and Tomato Bruschetta

Avocado and Tomato Bruschetta is a delicious and refreshing appetizer that combines the creaminess of avocado with the tanginess of tomatoes. This dish is perfect for summer gatherings or as a light snack. The combination of flavors and textures will surely impress your guests!
Serving: 4 servings
Preparation time: 10 minutes
Ready time: 15 minutes

Ingredients:
- 1 ripe avocado
- 2 medium tomatoes
- 1 small red onion
- 2 cloves of garlic
- 1 tablespoon of fresh lemon juice
- 2 tablespoons of fresh basil, chopped
- Salt and pepper to taste
- 4 slices of crusty bread

Instructions:
1. Start by preparing the avocado. Cut it in half, remove the pit, and scoop out the flesh into a bowl. Mash the avocado with a fork until it reaches a smooth consistency.
2. Dice the tomatoes and finely chop the red onion and garlic cloves. Add them to the bowl with the mashed avocado.
3. Add the fresh lemon juice, chopped basil, salt, and pepper to the bowl. Mix everything together until well combined.
4. Toast the slices of crusty bread until they are golden brown and crispy.
5. Once the bread is toasted, spread a generous amount of the avocado and tomato mixture on top of each slice.
6. Serve the avocado and tomato bruschetta immediately and enjoy!

Nutrition information:
- Calories: 180
- Fat: 8g

- Carbohydrates: 24g
- Protein: 5g
- Fiber: 6g
- Sugar: 4g
- Sodium: 250mg

Note: Nutrition information may vary depending on the specific Ingredients and quantities used.

20. Avocado and Turkey Club Sandwich

This Avocado and Turkey Club Sandwich is a satisfying and delicious meal that has all the flavors of a traditional club sandwich with added nutrition from the creamy avocado. Made with toasted wheat bread, turkey, bacon, lettuce, tomato, and avocado, this sandwich comes together in a few easy steps and is a great choice for an easy lunch or dinner.

Serving: 4
Preparation time: 15 minutes
Ready time: 15 minutes

Ingredients:
- 8 slices of wheat bread
- 3 ounces of cooked turkey, sliced
- 6 slices of cooked bacon
- 1/2 ripe avocado, sliced
- 2 lettuce leaves
- 2 tomato slices
- Mayonnaise

Instructions:
1. Toast the wheat bread using either a toaster or a hot pan.
2. Spread mayonnaise onto 4 of the slices of toasted bread.
3. On top of the mayonnaise, layer turkey, bacon, lettuce, tomato, and avocado.
4. Top with the remaining slices of toasted wheat bread.
5. Cut the sandwich into four triangles and serve.

Nutrition information:

Serving size – 1 sandwich
Calories – 346 kcal
Fat – 17.4 g
Carbohydrates – 34.7 g
Protein – 15.2 g

21. Avocado and Lime Ice Cream

Avocado and Lime Ice Cream is a refreshing and creamy dessert that combines the rich and buttery flavor of avocados with the tangy and zesty taste of lime. This unique combination creates a delightful treat that is perfect for hot summer days or any time you crave a cool and creamy dessert. With just a few simple Ingredients and minimal effort, you can whip up this delicious ice cream in no time.
Serving: 4 servings
Preparation time: 10 minutes
Ready time: 4-6 hours (including freezing time)

Ingredients:
- 2 ripe avocados
- 1 cup heavy cream
- 1/2 cup whole milk
- 1/2 cup granulated sugar
- Zest and juice of 2 limes
- 1 teaspoon vanilla extract

Instructions:
1. Cut the avocados in half, remove the pits, and scoop out the flesh into a blender or food processor.
2. Add the heavy cream, whole milk, granulated sugar, lime zest, lime juice, and vanilla extract to the blender or food processor.
3. Blend or process the mixture until smooth and creamy, ensuring there are no lumps of avocado remaining.
4. Pour the mixture into an ice cream maker and churn according to the manufacturer's instructions until it reaches a soft-serve consistency.
5. Transfer the ice cream to a lidded container and freeze for at least 4-6 hours, or until firm.

6. Once the ice cream is fully frozen, scoop it into bowls or cones and serve immediately.

Nutrition information per Serving: - Calories: 320
- Fat: 25g
- Carbohydrates: 23g
- Protein: 3g
- Fiber: 5g
- Sugar: 16g
- Sodium: 20mg

Note: Nutrition information may vary depending on the specific Ingredients and brands used.

22. Avocado and Bacon Deviled Eggs

Avocado and Bacon Deviled Eggs are a delicious twist on the classic deviled eggs. Creamy avocado and crispy bacon add a burst of flavor to these bite-sized appetizers. They are perfect for parties, potlucks, or as a tasty snack. Get ready to impress your guests with this simple yet impressive recipe!
Serving: 12 deviled eggs
Preparation time: 15 minutes
Ready time: 30 minutes

Ingredients:
- 6 hard-boiled eggs
- 1 ripe avocado
- 2 slices of bacon, cooked and crumbled
- 2 tablespoons mayonnaise
- 1 tablespoon Dijon mustard
- 1 tablespoon fresh lemon juice
- Salt and pepper to taste
- Paprika, for garnish
- Fresh chives, chopped (optional, for garnish)

Instructions:
1. Cut the hard-boiled eggs in half lengthwise. Carefully remove the yolks and place them in a bowl.

2. Mash the avocado and add it to the bowl with the egg yolks.
3. Add the crumbled bacon, mayonnaise, Dijon mustard, and lemon juice to the bowl. Mix well until all the Ingredients are combined and creamy. Season with salt and pepper to taste.
4. Spoon the avocado and bacon mixture into the egg white halves, dividing it evenly among them.
5. Sprinkle each deviled egg with a pinch of paprika for added flavor and a pop of color.
6. If desired, garnish with chopped fresh chives for an extra touch of freshness.
7. Chill the deviled eggs in the refrigerator for at least 15 minutes before serving to allow the flavors to meld together.
8. Serve chilled and enjoy!

Nutrition information per Serving: - Calories: 85
- Fat: 7g
- Protein: 4g
- Carbohydrates: 1g
- Fiber: 1g
- Sugar: 0g
- Sodium: 120mg

Note: Nutrition information may vary depending on the specific Ingredients and brands used.

23. Avocado and Pesto Pasta

This vibrant and flavorful Avocado and Pesto Pasta is a great way to enjoy a healthy and delicious meal in just a few minutes.
Serving: Serves 4
Preparation time: 10 minutes
Ready time: 15 minutes

Ingredients:
- 1/2 lb (250 grams) spaghetti
- 2 ripe avocados
- 2 cloves garlic
- 1/2 cup (120 ml) basil pesto
- 2 tablespoons olive oil

- 2 tablespoons lemon juice
- Salt and pepper to taste

Instructions:
1. Bring a large pot of lightly salted water to a boil and cook the spaghetti until al dente, about 8 minutes.
2. In the meantime, mash the avocados with a fork and add the crushed garlic, pesto, olive oil, lemon juice, salt and pepper. Stir until well combined.
3. Drain the cooked spaghetti and return it to the pot.
4. Pour the avocado mixture over the spaghetti and mix until well combined.
5. Serve the pasta hot, garnished with some fresh basil if desired.

Nutrition information
Calories: 504
Fat: 27 g
Carbohydrates: 59 g
Protein: 11 g

24. Avocado and Roasted Red Pepper Hummus Wrap

This Avocado and Roasted Red Pepper Hummus Wrap is a delicious and healthy option for a quick and satisfying meal. Packed with nutritious Ingredients and bursting with flavors, this wrap is perfect for lunch or a light dinner. The combination of creamy avocado, smoky roasted red pepper hummus, and fresh vegetables makes this wrap a true delight for your taste buds.
Serving: 2 wraps
Preparation time: 15 minutes
Ready time: 15 minutes

Ingredients:
- 2 large tortilla wraps
- 1 ripe avocado, sliced
- 1/2 cup roasted red pepper hummus
- 1/2 cup shredded lettuce

- 1/4 cup sliced cucumber
- 1/4 cup sliced red onion
- 1/4 cup sliced black olives
- Salt and pepper to taste

Instructions:
1. Lay the tortilla wraps flat on a clean surface.
2. Spread a generous amount of roasted red pepper hummus evenly over each tortilla.
3. Place the sliced avocado on top of the hummus, dividing it equally between the two wraps.
4. Sprinkle shredded lettuce, sliced cucumber, red onion, and black olives over the avocado.
5. Season with salt and pepper to taste.
6. Roll up the wraps tightly, tucking in the sides as you go.
7. Slice the wraps in half diagonally and serve.

Nutrition information per Serving: - Calories: 320
- Fat: 15g
- Carbohydrates: 40g
- Fiber: 8g
- Protein: 8g
- Sodium: 480mg

Note: Nutrition information may vary depending on the specific brands and quantities of Ingredients used.

25. Avocado and Black Bean Burritos

Avocado and Black Bean Burritos are a delicious and nutritious meal option that is perfect for lunch or dinner. Packed with protein, fiber, and healthy fats, these burritos are not only satisfying but also incredibly flavorful. The combination of creamy avocado and hearty black beans creates a filling and tasty filling that will leave you wanting more. Whether you're a vegetarian or simply looking for a meatless meal option, these burritos are sure to become a favorite in your household.
Serving: 4 burritos
Preparation time: 15 minutes
Ready time: 25 minutes

Ingredients:
- 4 large flour tortillas
- 1 cup cooked black beans
- 1 ripe avocado, sliced
- 1/2 cup diced tomatoes
- 1/4 cup diced red onion
- 1/4 cup chopped fresh cilantro
- 1/4 cup shredded cheddar cheese (optional)
- 1/4 cup sour cream (optional)
- Salt and pepper to taste

Instructions:
1. Warm the flour tortillas in a dry skillet over medium heat for about 30 seconds on each side, or until they become pliable. Set aside.
2. In a medium bowl, mash the black beans with a fork until they become slightly chunky. Season with salt and pepper to taste.
3. Lay one tortilla flat on a clean surface. Spread a quarter of the mashed black beans onto the center of the tortilla, leaving a border around the edges.
4. Top the black beans with a few slices of avocado, diced tomatoes, red onion, and chopped cilantro. If desired, sprinkle some shredded cheddar cheese on top.
5. Fold the sides of the tortilla over the filling, then roll it up tightly from the bottom to form a burrito. Repeat with the remaining tortillas and filling.
6. Optional: Heat a large skillet over medium heat and lightly coat it with cooking spray. Place the burritos seam-side down in the skillet and cook for 2-3 minutes on each side, or until they become golden brown and crispy.
7. Serve the avocado and black bean burritos warm, with a dollop of sour cream on top if desired.

Nutrition information per Serving: - Calories: 350
- Fat: 12g
- Carbohydrates: 48g
- Fiber: 10g
- Protein: 12g

26. Avocado and Shrimp Salad

Enjoy the refreshing and crunchy flavor of this Avocado and Shrimp Salad. With just a few simple Ingredients and minimal time and effort, this tasty salad makes a perfect light meal or side dish that will be sure to impress!
Serving: Serves 4
Preparation time: 10 minutes
Ready time: 10 minutes

Ingredients:
- 4oz cooked shrimp, sliced or diced
- 2 avocados, diced
- 1 ½ cups cherry tomatoes, halved
- ¼ cup red onion, finely diced
- 2 tablespoons extra virgin olive oil
- 2 tablespoons freshly squeezed lemon juice
- 2 tablespoons finely chopped fresh cilantro
- Salt and pepper to taste

Instructions:
1. In a large bowl, combine the shrimp, avocados, cherry tomatoes, and red onion.
2. In a separate small bowl, whisk together the olive oil, lemon juice, cilantro, salt, and pepper.
3. Pour the dressing over the salad and mix until everything is evenly coated.
4. Serve the salad chilled or at room temperature.

Nutrition information:
Calories: 282; Total Fat: 17g; Saturated Fat: 2.5g; Cholesterol: 103mg; Sodium: 285mg; Total Carbohydrates: 15g; Dietary Fiber: 3.3g; Protein: 14.2g

27. Avocado and Sweet Potato Hash

Avocado and Sweet Potato Hash is a delicious and nutritious dish that combines the creaminess of avocado with the sweetness of sweet potatoes. This hearty and flavorful hash is perfect for breakfast or brunch and will leave you feeling satisfied and energized for the day ahead.

Serving: 4 servings
Preparation time: 10 minutes
Ready time: 30 minutes

Ingredients:
- 2 large sweet potatoes, peeled and diced
- 1 red bell pepper, diced
- 1 small red onion, diced
- 2 cloves of garlic, minced
- 2 tablespoons olive oil
- 1 teaspoon paprika
- 1/2 teaspoon cumin
- Salt and pepper to taste
- 2 ripe avocados, diced
- Fresh cilantro, chopped (for garnish)

Instructions:
1. In a large skillet, heat the olive oil over medium heat. Add the diced sweet potatoes and cook for about 10 minutes, or until they start to soften.
2. Add the diced red bell pepper, red onion, and minced garlic to the skillet. Cook for an additional 5 minutes, or until the vegetables are tender.
3. Sprinkle the paprika, cumin, salt, and pepper over the vegetables. Stir well to evenly coat the sweet potatoes and peppers with the spices. Cook for another 2 minutes to allow the flavors to meld together.
4. Remove the skillet from the heat and gently fold in the diced avocados. Be careful not to mash the avocados too much, as you want to keep some texture.
5. Serve the avocado and sweet potato hash hot, garnished with fresh cilantro.

Nutrition information per Serving: - Calories: 250
- Fat: 15g
- Carbohydrates: 28g
- Fiber: 8g
- Protein: 4g

Note: Nutrition information may vary depending on the specific Ingredients and brands used.

28. Avocado and Grilled Vegetable Panini

Avocado and Grilled Vegetable Panini is a delicious and healthy sandwich that is perfect for a quick and satisfying meal. Packed with nutritious Ingredients and bursting with flavors, this panini is a great option for both vegetarians and meat-lovers alike. The combination of creamy avocado, grilled vegetables, and melted cheese makes this sandwich a true delight. Whether you're looking for a light lunch or a tasty dinner, this recipe is sure to please your taste buds.
Serving: 2 servings
Preparation time: 15 minutes
Ready time: 25 minutes

Ingredients:
- 1 large avocado, sliced
- 1 medium zucchini, sliced lengthwise
- 1 red bell pepper, sliced
- 1 small red onion, sliced
- 4 slices of whole grain bread
- 4 slices of mozzarella cheese
- 2 tablespoons of olive oil
- Salt and pepper to taste

Instructions:
1. Preheat your grill or grill pan over medium heat.
2. In a bowl, toss the zucchini, red bell pepper, and red onion with olive oil, salt, and pepper.
3. Place the vegetables on the grill and cook for about 5-7 minutes, or until they are tender and slightly charred. Flip them halfway through to ensure even cooking.
4. Remove the grilled vegetables from the heat and set aside.
5. Take two slices of bread and layer each with a slice of mozzarella cheese.
6. Top the cheese with a generous amount of sliced avocado.
7. Add the grilled vegetables on top of the avocado.

8. Place the remaining slices of bread on top to form sandwiches.
9. Lightly brush the outsides of the sandwiches with olive oil.
10. Heat a panini press or a large skillet over medium heat.
11. Place the sandwiches in the panini press or skillet and cook for about 3-4 minutes on each side, or until the bread is golden brown and the cheese is melted.
12. Remove the panini from the heat and let them cool for a minute before slicing them in half.
13. Serve the Avocado and Grilled Vegetable Panini warm and enjoy!

Nutrition information per Serving: - Calories: 380
- Fat: 22g
- Carbohydrates: 35g
- Fiber: 9g
- Protein: 15g

29. Avocado and Tomato Gazpacho

Avocado and Tomato Gazpacho is a refreshing and healthy cold soup that is perfect for hot summer days. Packed with the goodness of avocados and tomatoes, this gazpacho is not only delicious but also incredibly nutritious. It is a great way to incorporate fresh vegetables into your diet and can be enjoyed as a light lunch or a starter.
Serving: 4 servings
Preparation time: 15 minutes
Ready time: 2 hours (including chilling time)

Ingredients:
- 2 ripe avocados, peeled and pitted
- 4 medium-sized tomatoes, chopped
- 1 cucumber, peeled and chopped
- 1 small red onion, chopped
- 2 garlic cloves, minced
- 2 tablespoons fresh lime juice
- 2 tablespoons extra virgin olive oil
- 1 cup vegetable broth
- Salt and pepper to taste
- Fresh cilantro or basil leaves for garnish (optional)

Instructions:
1. In a blender or food processor, combine the avocados, tomatoes, cucumber, red onion, garlic, lime juice, olive oil, and vegetable broth. Blend until smooth and creamy.
2. Season with salt and pepper to taste. Adjust the lime juice and olive oil if needed.
3. Transfer the gazpacho to a large bowl or individual serving bowls. Cover and refrigerate for at least 2 hours to allow the flavors to meld together and the soup to chill.
4. Before serving, give the gazpacho a good stir. Garnish with fresh cilantro or basil leaves if desired.
5. Serve chilled and enjoy!

Nutrition information per Serving: - Calories: 180
- Fat: 14g
- Carbohydrates: 14g
- Fiber: 7g
- Protein: 3g
- Vitamin C: 30% of the daily recommended intake
- Vitamin A: 15% of the daily recommended intake
- Potassium: 480mg

30. Avocado and Feta Stuffed Portobello Mushrooms

Avocado and Feta Stuffed Portobello Mushrooms are a delicious and healthy vegetarian dish that is perfect for a light lunch or dinner. The combination of creamy avocado and tangy feta cheese stuffed into meaty portobello mushrooms creates a flavorful and satisfying meal. This recipe is quick and easy to make, making it a great option for busy weeknights or when you're craving a nutritious and tasty meal.
Serving: 4 servings
Preparation time: 15 minutes
Ready time: 25 minutes

Ingredients:
- 4 large portobello mushrooms
- 2 ripe avocados

- 1/2 cup crumbled feta cheese
- 1/4 cup chopped fresh parsley
- 2 tablespoons lemon juice
- 2 cloves garlic, minced
- Salt and pepper to taste
- Olive oil for brushing

Instructions:
1. Preheat your oven to 375°F (190°C). Line a baking sheet with parchment paper.
2. Remove the stems from the portobello mushrooms and gently scrape out the gills using a spoon. Place the mushrooms on the prepared baking sheet.
3. In a medium bowl, mash the avocados with a fork until smooth. Add the crumbled feta cheese, chopped parsley, lemon juice, minced garlic, salt, and pepper. Mix well to combine.
4. Spoon the avocado and feta mixture into the hollowed-out portobello mushrooms, dividing it evenly among them.
5. Brush the mushrooms with olive oil and season with additional salt and pepper if desired.
6. Bake the stuffed mushrooms in the preheated oven for 20-25 minutes, or until the mushrooms are tender and the filling is heated through.
7. Remove from the oven and let cool for a few minutes before serving.
8. Serve the avocado and feta stuffed portobello mushrooms as a main dish with a side salad or as a side dish alongside grilled chicken or fish.

Nutrition information per Serving: - Calories: 180
- Fat: 14g
- Carbohydrates: 10g
- Protein: 6g
- Fiber: 6g
- Sugar: 1g
- Sodium: 250mg

31. Avocado and Chicken Caesar Salad

Avocado and Chicken Caesar Salad is a delicious and nutritious dish that combines the creaminess of avocado with the savory flavors of chicken and Caesar dressing. This salad is perfect for a light lunch or dinner and is packed with protein and healthy fats. With its vibrant colors and refreshing taste, it's sure to become a favorite in your household.

Serving: 2 servings
Preparation time: 15 minutes
Ready time: 15 minutes

Ingredients:
- 2 boneless, skinless chicken breasts
- 1 ripe avocado, sliced
- 4 cups romaine lettuce, washed and torn into bite-sized pieces
- 1/4 cup grated Parmesan cheese
- 1/4 cup Caesar dressing
- 1/4 cup croutons
- Salt and pepper to taste

Instructions:
1. Preheat your grill or stovetop grill pan over medium-high heat.
2. Season the chicken breasts with salt and pepper on both sides.
3. Grill the chicken for about 6-8 minutes per side, or until cooked through and no longer pink in the center. Remove from heat and let it rest for a few minutes.
4. Slice the grilled chicken into thin strips.
5. In a large salad bowl, combine the romaine lettuce, avocado slices, and sliced chicken.
6. Drizzle the Caesar dressing over the salad and toss gently to coat all the Ingredients.
7. Sprinkle the grated Parmesan cheese and croutons over the top of the salad.
8. Serve immediately and enjoy!

Nutrition information per Serving: - Calories: 350
- Fat: 20g
- Protein: 30g
- Carbohydrates: 12g
- Fiber: 6g
- Sugar: 2g
- Sodium: 500mg

Note: Nutrition information may vary depending on the brand of Caesar dressing used.

32. Avocado and Strawberry Smoothie

This delicious and colorful Avocado and Strawberry Smoothie is filled with nutritious fruits and makes a great breakfast or snack.
Serving:
Makes 4 servings.
Preparation Time:
5 minutes
Ready Time:
5 minutes

Ingredients:
- ½ ripe avocado
- ½ cup of sliced strawberries
- 1 ripe banana
- ½ cup Greek yogurt
- 1 cup of almond milk
- 2 tablespoons of honey
- Ice

Instructions:
1. Place avocado, strawberries, banana, yogurt and almond milk in a blender.
2. Blend Ingredients until thick and creamy smoothie is achieved.
3. Add honey and ice and blend until it is mixed.
4. Pour the smoothie in glasses and serve.

Nutrition information:
Per Serving: Calories: 165; Total Fat: 6.3g; Cholesterol: 4mg; Sodium: 25mg; Total Carbohydrates: 24g; Protein: 4.6g; Sugar: 13.5g; Fiber: 4.2g; Iron: 0.4mg.

33. Avocado and Spinach Stuffed Chicken Breast

This Avocado and Spinach Stuffed Chicken Breast recipe is a delicious way to enjoy a hearty and flavorful dinner. The creamy avocado and

fresh spinach make a tasty combination when combined with succulent rotisserie chicken and melted shredded cheese.
Serving: Serves 4
Preparation time: 10 minutes
Ready time: 40 minutes

Ingredients:
- 4 boneless, skinless chicken breasts
- 2 cups cooked spinach, drained and patted dry
- 1 large avocado, mashed
- 8 slices provolone cheese
- 2 tablespoons olive oil

Instructions:
1. Pre-heat your oven to 375 degrees Fahrenheit.
2. Place the chicken breasts on a cutting surface. Cut a pocket in each chicken breast.
3. In a bowl, combine the drained cooked spinach and mashed avocado. Divide the spinach-avocado mixture into 4 portions. Stuff each chicken breast pocket with one portion of the mixture.
4. Place the stuffed chicken breasts in an oven safe dish. Top each with 2 slices of provolone cheese. Drizzle the chicken breasts with the olive oil.
5. Bake in the pre-heated oven for 30-35 minutes, or until the chicken breasts are cooked through and the cheese is melted and golden.

Nutrition information: Calories 312, Protein 28.6g, Total Carbohydrate 4.1g, Dietary Fibers 3.3g, Total Fat 17.3g, Saturated Fat 5.3g, Cholesterol 94.6 mg, Sodium 269.6 mg

34. Avocado and Quinoa Stuffed Bell Peppers

Avocado and Quinoa Stuffed Bell Peppers are a delicious and nutritious dish that combines the creaminess of avocado, the protein-packed quinoa, and the vibrant flavors of bell peppers. This recipe is perfect for a healthy lunch or dinner option that will leave you feeling satisfied and nourished.
Serving: 4 servings
Preparation time: 15 minutes

Ready time: 40 minutes

Ingredients:
- 4 bell peppers (any color)
- 1 cup cooked quinoa
- 2 ripe avocados, diced
- 1 small red onion, finely chopped
- 1 small tomato, diced
- 1/4 cup fresh cilantro, chopped
- 1/4 cup feta cheese, crumbled (optional)
- Juice of 1 lime
- Salt and pepper to taste

Instructions:
1. Preheat your oven to 375°F (190°C).
2. Cut the tops off the bell peppers and remove the seeds and membranes. Rinse them under cold water and set aside.
3. In a large mixing bowl, combine the cooked quinoa, diced avocados, chopped red onion, diced tomato, chopped cilantro, and crumbled feta cheese (if using).
4. Squeeze the lime juice over the mixture and season with salt and pepper to taste. Gently toss everything together until well combined.
5. Stuff each bell pepper with the quinoa and avocado mixture, pressing it down gently to fill the peppers completely.
6. Place the stuffed bell peppers on a baking sheet and bake in the preheated oven for 25-30 minutes, or until the peppers are tender and slightly charred.
7. Remove from the oven and let them cool for a few minutes before serving.
8. Garnish with additional chopped cilantro, if desired, and serve warm.

Nutrition information per Serving: - Calories: 250
- Fat: 12g
- Carbohydrates: 30g
- Fiber: 9g
- Protein: 7g
- Sodium: 200mg

Note: Nutrition information may vary depending on the specific Ingredients and brands used.

35. Avocado and Bacon Pasta Salad

Avocado and Bacon Pasta Salad is a delicious and refreshing dish that combines the creaminess of avocado with the smoky flavor of bacon. This salad is perfect for a light lunch or as a side dish for a barbecue or picnic. With its vibrant colors and flavors, it is sure to be a hit with everyone!

Serving: 4 servings
Preparation time: 15 minutes
Ready time: 30 minutes

Ingredients:
- 8 ounces of pasta (any shape you prefer)
- 4 slices of bacon, cooked and crumbled
- 2 ripe avocados, diced
- 1 cup cherry tomatoes, halved
- 1/4 cup red onion, finely chopped
- 1/4 cup fresh cilantro, chopped
- 2 tablespoons lime juice
- 2 tablespoons olive oil
- Salt and pepper to taste

Instructions:
1. Cook the pasta according to the package instructions until al dente. Drain and rinse with cold water to stop the cooking process. Set aside.
2. In a large bowl, combine the diced avocados, cherry tomatoes, red onion, and cilantro.
3. In a small bowl, whisk together the lime juice, olive oil, salt, and pepper.
4. Add the cooked pasta and crumbled bacon to the avocado mixture. Pour the dressing over the salad and gently toss to combine.
5. Adjust the seasoning if needed and refrigerate for at least 15 minutes to allow the flavors to meld together.
6. Serve chilled and enjoy!

Nutrition information per Serving: - Calories: 350
- Fat: 18g
- Carbohydrates: 38g

- Protein: 10g
- Fiber: 6g

36. Avocado and Tofu Stir-Fry

This delicious vegan stir- fry is perfect for any occasion or special diet. Avocado and tofu come together to create a flavorful and nutritious dish that will be sure to become one of your favorites.

Serving: 4
Preparation time: 10 minutes
Ready time: 25 minutes

Ingredients:
- 1/2 block of firm tofu, cut into small cubes
- 2 avocados, halved and cubed
- 1/4 cup vegetable broth
- 2 tablespoons soy sauce
- 2 teaspoons sesame oil
- 1 teaspoon fresh ginger, grated
- 2 cloves garlic, minced
- 1/2 teaspoon red pepper flakes
- 2 cups bok choy, finely chopped
- 2 tablespoons olive oil
- Salt and pepper to taste

Instructions:
1. Heat 1 tablespoon of olive oil in a skillet over medium-high heat.
2. Once the oil is hot, add the cubed tofu and cook until lightly browned, about 5 minutes.
3. Add the remaining 1 tablespoon of olive oil, the ginger, garlic, and red pepper flakes. Cook for an additional 2 minutes.
4. Add the bok choy and cook for 5 minutes, stirring frequently.
5. Add the avocado and vegetable broth. Cook for an additional 3 minutes.
6. Finish by stirring in the soy sauce, sesame oil, salt, and pepper.
7. Serve over steamed rice or quinoa.

Nutrition information: Per Serving - 274 calories, 17 g fat (3 g saturated fat), 11 g carbohydrates, 3.2 g sugar, 8 g protein, 4.1 g fiber, 180 mg sodium.

37. Avocado and Corn Chowder

Avocado and Corn Chowder is a delicious and creamy soup that combines the rich flavors of avocado and sweet corn. This hearty dish is perfect for a cozy dinner or a comforting lunch. Packed with nutrients and bursting with flavor, this chowder is sure to become a favorite in your household.
Serving: 4 servings
Preparation time: 15 minutes
Ready time: 30 minutes

Ingredients:
- 2 ripe avocados, peeled and pitted
- 2 cups frozen corn kernels
- 1 onion, diced
- 2 cloves garlic, minced
- 2 tablespoons olive oil
- 4 cups vegetable broth
- 1 cup milk (or dairy-free alternative)
- 1 teaspoon cumin
- 1 teaspoon paprika
- Salt and pepper to taste
- Fresh cilantro, chopped (for garnish)

Instructions:
1. In a large pot, heat the olive oil over medium heat. Add the diced onion and minced garlic, and sauté until the onion becomes translucent and fragrant.
2. Add the frozen corn kernels to the pot and cook for a few minutes until they are heated through.
3. In a blender or food processor, combine one avocado with 1 cup of vegetable broth. Blend until smooth and creamy.
4. Pour the avocado mixture into the pot with the corn and onion. Stir well to combine.

5. Add the remaining vegetable broth, cumin, paprika, salt, and pepper to the pot. Stir to combine all the Ingredients.
6. Bring the chowder to a simmer and let it cook for about 15 minutes, allowing the flavors to meld together.
7. While the chowder is simmering, dice the second avocado into small cubes for garnish.
8. After 15 minutes, remove the pot from the heat and stir in the milk. Adjust the seasoning if needed.
9. Ladle the avocado and corn chowder into bowls and top with the diced avocado and fresh cilantro.
10. Serve hot and enjoy!

Nutrition information per Serving: - Calories: 280
- Fat: 18g
- Carbohydrates: 27g
- Fiber: 7g
- Protein: 6g

38. Avocado and Goat Cheese Crostini

Avocado and Goat Cheese Crostini is a delightful appetizer that combines the creamy richness of avocado with the tangy flavor of goat cheese. This dish is perfect for entertaining guests or enjoying as a light snack. The crostini bread adds a satisfying crunch, while the combination of flavors creates a mouthwatering experience.
Serving: 4 servings
Preparation time: 10 minutes
Ready time: 15 minutes

Ingredients:
- 1 ripe avocado
- 4 ounces goat cheese
- 1 French baguette
- 2 tablespoons olive oil
- 1 clove garlic, minced
- Salt and pepper to taste
- Fresh basil leaves, for garnish (optional)

Instructions:
1. Preheat the oven to 375°F (190°C).
2. Slice the baguette into 1/2-inch thick slices and arrange them on a baking sheet.
3. In a small bowl, combine the olive oil and minced garlic. Brush the mixture onto both sides of each bread slice.
4. Bake the bread slices in the preheated oven for about 10 minutes, or until they are golden and crispy. Remove from the oven and let them cool slightly.
5. While the bread is toasting, cut the avocado in half, remove the pit, and scoop out the flesh into a bowl. Mash the avocado with a fork until it reaches a smooth consistency.
6. In a separate bowl, crumble the goat cheese.
7. Spread a generous amount of mashed avocado onto each toasted bread slice.
8. Sprinkle the crumbled goat cheese on top of the avocado.
9. Season with salt and pepper to taste.
10. If desired, garnish each crostini with a fresh basil leaf.
11. Serve immediately and enjoy!

Nutrition information per Serving: - Calories: 220
- Fat: 12g
- Carbohydrates: 21g
- Protein: 7g
- Fiber: 3g

39. Avocado and Tomato Omelette

Avocado and Tomato Omelette is a delicious and nutritious breakfast option that combines the creaminess of avocado with the freshness of tomatoes. This omelette is packed with protein and healthy fats, making it a perfect way to start your day. With its vibrant colors and flavors, this dish is sure to impress your taste buds.
Serving: 1 omelette
Preparation time: 10 minutes
Ready time: 15 minutes

Ingredients:

- 2 large eggs
- 1/4 cup diced tomatoes
- 1/4 cup diced avocado
- 1/4 cup shredded cheddar cheese
- 1 tablespoon chopped fresh cilantro
- Salt and pepper to taste
- 1 tablespoon olive oil

Instructions:
1. In a bowl, whisk the eggs until well beaten. Season with salt and pepper.
2. Heat the olive oil in a non-stick skillet over medium heat.
3. Pour the beaten eggs into the skillet and let them cook for about 2 minutes, or until the edges start to set.
4. Sprinkle the diced tomatoes, avocado, shredded cheddar cheese, and chopped cilantro evenly over one half of the omelette.
5. Using a spatula, carefully fold the other half of the omelette over the filling.
6. Cook for another 2-3 minutes, or until the cheese has melted and the omelette is cooked through.
7. Slide the omelette onto a plate and garnish with additional chopped cilantro, if desired.

Nutrition information:
- Calories: 320
- Protein: 18g
- Fat: 24g
- Carbohydrates: 7g
- Fiber: 4g
- Sugar: 2g
- Sodium: 320mg

Note: Nutrition information may vary depending on the size of the eggs and the amount of cheese used.

40. Avocado and Black Bean Salsa

Try something new for your next dinner party or potluck with this Avocado and Black Bean Salsa recipe. It is a flavorful and healthy

combination of mashed avocados, black beans, tomatoes, and spices, served with your favorite type of chips.
Serving: 6-8
Preparation time: 10 mins
Ready Time: 10 mins

Ingredients:
-2 avocados, peeled, pitted and mashed
-1 (15-ounce) can black beans, drained and rinsed
-1 cup diced tomatoes
-1/4 cup diced onion
-1/4 cup chopped fresh cilantro
-2 tablespoons lime juice
-1 teaspoon garlic salt
-1/4 teaspoon ground black pepper

Instructions:
1. In a medium size bowl, combine mashed avocados, black beans, tomatoes, onion, cilantro, lime juice, garlic salt, and pepper.
2. Mix well and chill the salsa for about 30 minutes, to allow flavors to blend.
3. Serve with tortilla chips or use to top off your favorite dishes.

Nutrition information: Serving size: 1/6 of the recipe | Calories: 94 kcal | Fat: 4.6g | Sodium: 147mg | Potassium: 282mg | Carbohydrates: 12.3g | Fiber: 4.9g | Protein: 3.7g

41. Avocado and Basil Pesto Pizza

This Avocado and Basil Pesto Pizza is a delicious and healthy pizza made with fresh Ingredients like avocados, basil pesto, pizza dough, and low-fat cheese. It's the perfect meal for any occasion.
Serving: 4
Preparation time: 10 mins
Ready time: 20 mins

Ingredients:
- 1 pre-made pizza dough or 2 purchased crusts

- 2 tablespoons basil pesto
- 1 avocado, peeled and sliced
- 1/2 cup low-fat mozzarella cheese
- 1/4 cup Parmesan cheese
- Salt and pepper to taste

Instructions:
1. Preheat the oven to 400°F (200°C).
2. Roll the pizza dough out to the desired thickness.
3. Spread the basil pesto over the dough.
4. Layer the avocado slices on top of the pesto.
5. Top the pizza with mozzarella cheese and sprinkle with Parmesan cheese.
6. Bake in the preheated oven for about 15 minutes, or until the cheese is melted and the crust is golden.
7. Remove from the oven and let cool before slicing and serving.

Nutrition information: Per serving – Calories: 224; Total Fat: 9.8g; Cholesterol: 10.8mg; Sodium: 224mg; Total Carbohydrates: 22.2g; Sugar: 0.3g; Protein: 11.2g

42. Avocado and Smoked Salmon Salad

This Avocado and Smoked Salmon Salad is a perfect combination of light and easy-to-make Ingredients that will make a delicious, healthy dinner for the whole family.
Serving: 4
Preparation Time: 15 minutes
Ready Time: 15 minutes

Ingredients:
- 4 large avocados
- 4 smoked salmon slices
- 1 cup watercress leaves
- Juice of 1 lemon
- 2 tablespoons olive oil
- Salt and freshly ground pepper, to taste

Instructions:
1. Peel and pit avocados. Cut them into cubes.
2. Place cubes in a large bowl and gently mix with smoked salmon slices and watercress leaves.
3. In a separate bowl, combine lemon juice, olive oil, salt and pepper and whisk until blended.
4. Pour dressing over the avocado salad and mix gently.

Nutrition information:
Serving Size: 1/4 of recipe
Calories: 207, Total Fat: 13g, Saturated Fat: 2g, Cholesterol: 7mg, Sodium: 137mg, Carbohydrates: 12g, Fiber: 8g, Protein: 12g

43. Avocado and Cucumber Soup

Avocado and Cucumber Soup is a refreshing and creamy soup that is perfect for hot summer days. Packed with healthy fats from avocados and the crispness of cucumbers, this soup is not only delicious but also nutritious. It can be served as a light appetizer or a refreshing main course.
Serving: 4 servings
Preparation time: 15 minutes
Ready time: 1 hour

Ingredients:
- 2 ripe avocados
- 1 large cucumber, peeled and diced
- 1 cup plain Greek yogurt
- 1 cup vegetable broth
- 1 garlic clove, minced
- 2 tablespoons fresh lime juice
- 1 tablespoon chopped fresh cilantro
- Salt and pepper to taste
- Optional toppings: diced tomatoes, chopped green onions, and a drizzle of olive oil

Instructions:

1. In a blender or food processor, combine the avocados, cucumber, Greek yogurt, vegetable broth, minced garlic, lime juice, and cilantro. Blend until smooth and creamy.
2. Season with salt and pepper to taste. If the soup is too thick, add more vegetable broth or water to achieve the desired consistency.
3. Transfer the soup to a bowl and refrigerate for at least 1 hour to allow the flavors to meld together.
4. Before serving, give the soup a good stir. Taste and adjust the seasoning if needed.
5. Ladle the chilled soup into bowls and garnish with diced tomatoes, chopped green onions, and a drizzle of olive oil, if desired.
6. Serve immediately and enjoy the refreshing flavors of avocado and cucumber.

Nutrition information per Serving: - Calories: 180
- Fat: 12g
- Carbohydrates: 14g
- Fiber: 7g
- Protein: 8g
- Sodium: 350mg

44. Avocado and Chicken Lettuce Wraps

Enjoy a fresh and healthy lunch with these easy-to-make Avocado and Chicken Lettuce Wraps! This tasty combination of chicken, avocado, bell peppers, and balsamic vinaigrette dressing wrapped in lettuce is sure to please.
Serving: 4
Preparation time: 10 minutes
Ready time: 10 minutes

Ingredients:
- 2 chicken breasts, cooked and diced
- 1 avocado, diced
- 1 red bell pepper, diced
- 1/4 cup balsamic vinaigrette dressing
- 4 lettuce leaves

Instructions:
1. Heat a skillet over medium heat.
2. Add the diced chicken, avocado, and bell pepper.
3. Sauté for 5 minutes, stirring occasionally.
4. Remove from heat and cool.
5. In a bowl, combine the cooled chicken, avocado, bell pepper, and balsamic vinaigrette dressing.
6. Spoon the mixture onto the lettuce leaves and roll up.
7. Serve and enjoy!

Nutrition information:
Calories: 212 per wrap
Fat: 12.4 g
Carbohydrates: 13.2 g
Protein: 10.2 g

45. Avocado and Lime Pound Cake

Avocado and Lime Pound Cake is a delightful twist on the classic pound cake. The addition of creamy avocado and tangy lime gives this cake a unique and refreshing flavor. It's perfect for any occasion, whether you're serving it as a dessert or enjoying it with a cup of tea. Get ready to indulge in a slice of this moist and flavorful cake!
Serving: 10-12 slices
Preparation time: 20 minutes
Ready time: 1 hour 30 minutes

Ingredients:
- 1 ½ cups all-purpose flour
- 1 teaspoon baking powder
- ½ teaspoon baking soda
- ¼ teaspoon salt
- ½ cup unsalted butter, softened
- 1 cup granulated sugar
- 2 ripe avocados, peeled and pitted
- Zest of 1 lime
- 2 tablespoons fresh lime juice
- 3 large eggs

- ½ cup sour cream
- 1 teaspoon vanilla extract

Instructions:
1. Preheat your oven to 350°F (175°C). Grease and flour a 9x5-inch loaf pan.
2. In a medium bowl, whisk together the flour, baking powder, baking soda, and salt. Set aside.
3. In a large mixing bowl, cream together the softened butter and granulated sugar until light and fluffy.
4. In a separate bowl, mash the avocados until smooth. Add the mashed avocados, lime zest, and lime juice to the butter mixture. Mix well.
5. Beat in the eggs, one at a time, ensuring each egg is fully incorporated before adding the next.
6. Add the sour cream and vanilla extract to the mixture and mix until well combined.
7. Gradually add the dry Ingredients to the wet Ingredients, mixing until just combined. Be careful not to overmix.
8. Pour the batter into the prepared loaf pan and smooth the top with a spatula.
9. Bake for 55-60 minutes, or until a toothpick inserted into the center comes out clean.
10. Remove the cake from the oven and let it cool in the pan for 10 minutes. Then, transfer it to a wire rack to cool completely.
11. Once cooled, slice and serve. Enjoy!

Nutrition information (per serving):
- Calories: 280
- Fat: 15g
- Carbohydrates: 33g
- Protein: 4g
- Fiber: 2g
- Sugar: 18g
- Sodium: 160mg

46. Avocado and Bacon Breakfast Burrito

Start your day off right with this delicious and satisfying Avocado and Bacon Breakfast Burrito. Packed with creamy avocado, crispy bacon, and a variety of flavorful Ingredients, this burrito is the perfect way to fuel your morning. Whether you're enjoying it at home or on the go, this recipe is sure to become a breakfast favorite.

Serving: 1 burrito
Preparation time: 10 minutes
Ready time: 15 minutes

Ingredients:
- 2 slices of bacon
- 2 large eggs
- Salt and pepper to taste
- 1 large tortilla
- 1/2 avocado, sliced
- 1/4 cup shredded cheddar cheese
- 2 tablespoons salsa
- Optional toppings: sour cream, chopped cilantro, hot sauce

Instructions:
1. In a skillet over medium heat, cook the bacon until crispy. Remove from the skillet and set aside on a paper towel-lined plate to drain excess grease.
2. In the same skillet, crack the eggs and season with salt and pepper. Scramble the eggs until cooked to your desired consistency.
3. Warm the tortilla in the skillet or microwave for a few seconds to make it pliable.
4. Lay the tortilla flat and arrange the sliced avocado, cooked bacon, scrambled eggs, shredded cheddar cheese, and salsa in the center of the tortilla.
5. Fold the sides of the tortilla over the filling, then roll it up tightly from the bottom to create a burrito shape.
6. Optional: If desired, lightly toast the burrito in a skillet or wrap it in foil and heat in the oven for a few minutes to melt the cheese.
7. Serve the Avocado and Bacon Breakfast Burrito immediately with optional toppings such as sour cream, chopped cilantro, or hot sauce.

Nutrition information:
- Calories: 450
- Fat: 30g

- Carbohydrates: 25g
- Protein: 20g
- Fiber: 5g
- Sugar: 2g
- Sodium: 600mg

Note: Nutrition information may vary depending on the specific brands and quantities of Ingredients used.

47. Avocado and Chickpea Stuffed Bell Peppers

Avocado and Chickpea Stuffed Bell Peppers are a delicious and nutritious dish that combines the creaminess of avocado with the protein-packed goodness of chickpeas. This recipe is not only easy to make but also a great option for a healthy and filling meal. The combination of flavors and textures in these stuffed bell peppers will surely satisfy your taste buds.

Serving: 4 servings
Preparation time: 15 minutes
Ready time: 30 minutes

Ingredients:
- 4 bell peppers (any color)
- 1 can (15 ounces) chickpeas, drained and rinsed
- 2 ripe avocados, peeled and diced
- 1 small red onion, finely chopped
- 1 small tomato, diced
- 1/4 cup fresh cilantro, chopped
- 2 tablespoons lime juice
- 1 tablespoon olive oil
- 1 teaspoon cumin
- Salt and pepper to taste

Instructions:
1. Preheat your oven to 375°F (190°C).
2. Cut the tops off the bell peppers and remove the seeds and membranes. Rinse them under cold water and set aside.

3. In a large bowl, combine the chickpeas, diced avocados, red onion, tomato, cilantro, lime juice, olive oil, cumin, salt, and pepper. Mix well until all the Ingredients are evenly combined.
4. Stuff each bell pepper with the avocado and chickpea mixture, pressing it down gently to fill the peppers completely.
5. Place the stuffed bell peppers on a baking sheet and bake in the preheated oven for 25-30 minutes, or until the peppers are tender and slightly charred.
6. Remove from the oven and let them cool for a few minutes before serving.
7. Serve the avocado and chickpea stuffed bell peppers as a main dish or as a side dish with your favorite salad or grain.

Nutrition information per Serving: - Calories: 250
- Fat: 12g
- Carbohydrates: 30g
- Fiber: 10g
- Protein: 8g
- Sodium: 150mg

48. Avocado and Shrimp Pasta

Avocado and Shrimp Pasta is a delicious and refreshing dish that combines the creaminess of avocado with the succulent taste of shrimp. This pasta dish is perfect for a quick and easy weeknight dinner or a special occasion. The combination of flavors and textures will leave you wanting more!
Serving: 4 servings
Preparation time: 15 minutes
Ready time: 30 minutes

Ingredients:
- 8 ounces of pasta (linguine or spaghetti)
- 1 ripe avocado, peeled and pitted
- 1/2 pound of shrimp, peeled and deveined
- 2 cloves of garlic, minced
- 1 tablespoon of olive oil
- 1/4 cup of fresh basil leaves, chopped

- 1/4 cup of grated Parmesan cheese
- Salt and pepper to taste

Instructions:
1. Cook the pasta according to the package instructions until al dente. Drain and set aside.
2. In a large skillet, heat the olive oil over medium heat. Add the minced garlic and sauté for about 1 minute until fragrant.
3. Add the shrimp to the skillet and cook for 3-4 minutes until they turn pink and opaque. Remove the shrimp from the skillet and set aside.
4. In a blender or food processor, combine the avocado, basil leaves, Parmesan cheese, salt, and pepper. Blend until smooth and creamy.
5. In the same skillet, add the cooked pasta and the avocado sauce. Toss until the pasta is well coated with the sauce.
6. Add the cooked shrimp to the skillet and gently toss to combine.
7. Serve the avocado and shrimp pasta hot, garnished with additional Parmesan cheese and basil leaves if desired.

Nutrition information per Serving: - Calories: 380
- Fat: 15g
- Carbohydrates: 40g
- Protein: 22g
- Fiber: 6g

49. Avocado and Tomato Quinoa Bowl

Avocado and Tomato Quinoa Bowl is a light yet satisfying vegan dish that is easy to make and incredibly healthy. This protein packed dish is full of flavor and makes a great lunch or dinner.
Serving: Serves 4
Preparation Time: 10 minutes
Ready Time: 20 minutes

Ingredients:
- 2 cups of cooked quinoa
- 2 tomatoes, diced
- 1 medium onion, diced
- 1 large avocado, cubed

- 2 cloves of garlic, minced
- Half a bunch of cilantro, chopped
- 2 tablespoons of olive oil
- Juice of half a lemon
- Salt and pepper to taste

Instructions:
1. Heat the olive oil in a large skillet over medium heat.
2. Add the onion and sauté for 5 minutes until softened.
3. Add the garlic and cook for another minute.
4. Add the tomatoes to the pan and cook for another 3-4 minutes.
5. Add the cooked quinoa to the pan and stir to combine.
6. Remove the pan from the heat and stir in the avocado, cilantro, lemon juice, salt, and pepper.
7. Serve warm or cold.

Nutrition information:
Calories: 184, Total fat: 9g, Saturated fat: 1g, Trans fat: 0g, Cholesterol: 0mg, Sodium: 82mg, Carbohydrate: 24g, Fiber: 6g, Sugars: 3g, Protein: 6g.

50. Avocado and Goat Cheese Stuffed Mushrooms

Avocado and Goat Cheese Stuffed Mushrooms are a delicious and healthy appetizer that will impress your guests. The combination of creamy avocado and tangy goat cheese creates a flavorful filling that pairs perfectly with the earthy taste of mushrooms. This recipe is quick and easy to make, making it a great option for any occasion.
Serving: 4 servings
Preparation time: 15 minutes
Ready time: 25 minutes

Ingredients:
- 12 large mushrooms
- 1 ripe avocado
- 4 ounces goat cheese
- 1 tablespoon lemon juice
- 2 tablespoons chopped fresh parsley

- Salt and pepper to taste

Instructions:
1. Preheat your oven to 375°F (190°C).
2. Remove the stems from the mushrooms and set them aside. Place the mushroom caps on a baking sheet lined with parchment paper.
3. In a medium bowl, mash the avocado with a fork until smooth. Add the goat cheese, lemon juice, chopped parsley, salt, and pepper. Mix well to combine.
4. Finely chop the mushroom stems and add them to the avocado and goat cheese mixture. Stir until evenly distributed.
5. Spoon the avocado and goat cheese mixture into the mushroom caps, filling each one generously.
6. Bake the stuffed mushrooms in the preheated oven for 20-25 minutes, or until the mushrooms are tender and the filling is golden brown.
7. Remove from the oven and let them cool for a few minutes before serving.

Nutrition information:
- Calories: 120
- Fat: 9g
- Carbohydrates: 5g
- Protein: 5g
- Fiber: 3g
- Sugar: 1g
- Sodium: 150mg

Note: Nutrition information may vary depending on the size of the mushrooms and the specific brands of Ingredients used.

51. Avocado and Cilantro Lime Dressing

Avocado and Cilantro Lime Dressing is a zesty and nutrient-packed dressing that will take any summer salad to the next level.
Serving: Makes 1-2 servings
Preparation Time: 5 minutes
Ready Time: 5 minutes

Ingredients:

- 1/4 cup plain Greek yogurt
- 1 ripe avocado
- 1/3 cup roughly chopped fresh cilantro
- Juice of 1 lime
- 1/4 teaspoon garlic powder
- Salt and pepper, to taste

Instructions:
1. In a medium-sized bowl, mash up the avocado with a fork until it becomes a paste.
2. Add the Greek yogurt, cilantro, lime juice, garlic powder, salt, and pepper, and stir with a spoon until everything is well combined.
3. Enjoy on top of a salad or in a wraps/burritos.

Nutrition information: 89 calories, 7 g fat, 5 g carbohydrates, 3 g protein

52. Avocado and Bacon Wrapped Shrimp

Avocado and Bacon Wrapped Shrimp is a mouthwatering appetizer that combines the creaminess of avocado with the smoky flavor of bacon and the succulent taste of shrimp. This dish is perfect for parties or as a delicious starter to any meal. The combination of these Ingredients creates a delightful explosion of flavors that will leave your taste buds wanting more.
Serving: 4 servings
Preparation time: 15 minutes
Ready time: 25 minutes

Ingredients:
- 16 large shrimp, peeled and deveined
- 8 slices of bacon, cut in half
- 2 ripe avocados, pitted and sliced
- 1 tablespoon olive oil
- 1 tablespoon lime juice
- 1 teaspoon garlic powder
- Salt and pepper to taste
- Toothpicks

Instructions:
1. Preheat your oven to 400°F (200°C) and line a baking sheet with parchment paper.
2. In a small bowl, combine the olive oil, lime juice, garlic powder, salt, and pepper. Mix well.
3. Place a slice of avocado on each shrimp and wrap it with a half slice of bacon. Secure the bacon with a toothpick.
4. Arrange the bacon-wrapped shrimp on the prepared baking sheet.
5. Brush the shrimp with the olive oil mixture, making sure to coat them evenly.
6. Bake in the preheated oven for 10-12 minutes, or until the bacon is crispy and the shrimp is cooked through.
7. Remove from the oven and let cool for a few minutes before serving.
8. Serve the avocado and bacon wrapped shrimp as an appetizer or alongside a fresh salad.

Nutrition information per Serving: - Calories: 250
- Fat: 18g
- Carbohydrates: 5g
- Protein: 18g
- Fiber: 3g

Note: Nutrition information may vary depending on the specific Ingredients and brands used.

53. Avocado and Black Bean Enchiladas

Avocado and Black Bean Enchiladas are a delicious and nutritious twist on traditional enchiladas. Packed with protein, fiber, and healthy fats, these enchiladas are not only satisfying but also good for you. The combination of creamy avocado, hearty black beans, and flavorful spices make this dish a crowd-pleaser. Whether you're a vegetarian or simply looking for a meatless meal option, these enchiladas are sure to become a favorite in your household.

Serving: 4 servings
Preparation time: 20 minutes
Ready time: 40 minutes

Ingredients:
- 8 small flour tortillas
- 2 ripe avocados, peeled and pitted
- 1 can (15 ounces) black beans, rinsed and drained
- 1 cup corn kernels (fresh or frozen)
- 1 small onion, diced
- 2 cloves garlic, minced
- 1 teaspoon ground cumin
- 1 teaspoon chili powder
- 1/2 teaspoon salt
- 1/4 teaspoon black pepper
- 1 cup shredded cheddar cheese
- 1 cup enchilada sauce
- Fresh cilantro, for garnish (optional)

Instructions:
1. Preheat your oven to 375°F (190°C). Grease a 9x13-inch baking dish and set aside.
2. In a large bowl, mash the avocados until smooth. Add the black beans, corn, onion, garlic, cumin, chili powder, salt, and black pepper. Stir well to combine.
3. Warm the tortillas in the microwave for about 30 seconds to make them more pliable. Spoon about 1/4 cup of the avocado and black bean mixture onto each tortilla, spreading it evenly down the center. Roll up the tortillas and place them seam-side down in the prepared baking dish.
4. Pour the enchilada sauce over the rolled tortillas, making sure to cover them completely. Sprinkle the shredded cheese on top.
5. Cover the baking dish with aluminum foil and bake for 20 minutes. Then, remove the foil and bake for an additional 10 minutes, or until the cheese is melted and bubbly.
6. Remove from the oven and let the enchiladas cool for a few minutes before serving. Garnish with fresh cilantro, if desired.
7. Serve the avocado and black bean enchiladas hot and enjoy!

Nutrition information per Serving: - Calories: 420
- Total Fat: 18g
- Saturated Fat: 6g
- Cholesterol: 20mg
- Sodium: 900mg
- Total Carbohydrate: 52g

- Dietary Fiber: 12g
- Sugars: 4g
- Protein: 16g

Note: Nutrition information may vary depending on the specific Ingredients and brands used.

54. Avocado and Tomato Grilled Cheese Sandwich

Avocado and Tomato Grilled Cheese Sandwich is a delicious twist on the classic grilled cheese sandwich. The creamy avocado and juicy tomato slices add a burst of flavor and freshness to this comforting dish. It's a perfect option for a quick and satisfying lunch or dinner.

Serving: 2 sandwiches
Preparation time: 10 minutes
Ready time: 15 minutes

Ingredients:
- 4 slices of bread (white, whole wheat, or your preferred choice)
- 1 ripe avocado, sliced
- 1 large tomato, sliced
- 4 slices of cheddar cheese
- Butter or margarine, softened

Instructions:
1. Preheat a skillet or griddle over medium heat.
2. Take two slices of bread and spread butter or margarine on one side of each slice.
3. Place one slice of bread, buttered side down, on the skillet or griddle.
4. Layer one slice of cheddar cheese, avocado slices, tomato slices, and another slice of cheddar cheese on top of the bread.
5. Place the second slice of bread, buttered side up, on top of the cheese.
6. Cook the sandwich for about 3-4 minutes on each side, or until the bread turns golden brown and the cheese melts.
7. Remove the sandwich from the skillet or griddle and let it cool for a minute.
8. Repeat the process with the remaining Ingredients to make the second sandwich.
9. Cut each sandwich in half and serve hot.

Nutrition information per Serving: - Calories: 420
- Fat: 25g
- Carbohydrates: 35g
- Protein: 15g
- Fiber: 8g
- Sugar: 5g
- Sodium: 550mg

Note: Nutrition information may vary depending on the type of bread and cheese used.

55. Avocado and Mango Smoothie

Avocado and Mango Smoothie is a refreshing and nutritious drink that combines the creamy goodness of avocado with the tropical sweetness of mango. Packed with vitamins, minerals, and healthy fats, this smoothie is not only delicious but also a great way to start your day or enjoy as a mid-day snack.

Serving: 2 servings
Preparation time: 5 minutes
Ready time: 5 minutes

Ingredients:
- 1 ripe avocado, peeled and pitted
- 1 ripe mango, peeled and diced
- 1 cup almond milk (or any milk of your choice)
- 1 tablespoon honey (optional, for added sweetness)
- Juice of 1 lime
- Ice cubes (optional, for a chilled smoothie)

Instructions:
1. In a blender, combine the avocado, mango, almond milk, honey (if using), and lime juice.
2. Blend on high speed until smooth and creamy. If desired, add a few ice cubes and blend again until well combined.
3. Taste the smoothie and adjust the sweetness by adding more honey if needed.
4. Pour the smoothie into glasses and serve immediately.

Nutrition information per Serving: - Calories: 220
- Fat: 10g
- Carbohydrates: 32g
- Fiber: 8g
- Protein: 3g
- Vitamin C: 60% of the daily recommended intake
- Vitamin A: 25% of the daily recommended intake
- Calcium: 20% of the daily recommended intake
- Iron: 10% of the daily recommended intake

Note: Nutrition information may vary depending on the specific Ingredients used.

56. Avocado and Spinach Stuffed Mushrooms

Avocado and Spinach Stuffed Mushrooms are a delicious and healthy appetizer that is perfect for any occasion. The combination of creamy avocado, nutritious spinach, and savory mushrooms creates a mouthwatering dish that will impress your guests. These stuffed mushrooms are not only easy to make but also packed with flavor and nutrients. Whether you are hosting a party or simply looking for a tasty snack, these stuffed mushrooms are sure to be a hit!

Serving: 4 servings
Preparation time: 15 minutes
Ready time: 25 minutes

Ingredients:
- 8 large mushrooms
- 1 ripe avocado
- 1 cup fresh spinach, chopped
- 1/4 cup grated Parmesan cheese
- 1/4 teaspoon garlic powder
- 1/4 teaspoon onion powder
- Salt and pepper to taste

Instructions:
1. Preheat your oven to 375°F (190°C).

2. Remove the stems from the mushrooms and set them aside. Place the mushroom caps on a baking sheet lined with parchment paper.
3. In a medium-sized bowl, mash the avocado until smooth.
4. Add the chopped spinach, grated Parmesan cheese, garlic powder, onion powder, salt, and pepper to the bowl with the mashed avocado. Mix well until all the Ingredients are combined.
5. Spoon the avocado and spinach mixture into the mushroom caps, filling them generously.
6. Finely chop the mushroom stems and sprinkle them over the stuffed mushrooms.
7. Bake the stuffed mushrooms in the preheated oven for 20-25 minutes, or until the mushrooms are tender and the filling is golden brown.
8. Remove from the oven and let them cool for a few minutes before serving.

Nutrition information:
- Calories: 120
- Fat: 8g
- Carbohydrates: 8g
- Protein: 5g
- Fiber: 4g
- Sugar: 1g
- Sodium: 150mg

Note: Nutrition information may vary depending on the size of the mushrooms and the specific brands of Ingredients used.

57. Avocado and Quinoa Salad

Avocado and Quinoa Salad is a refreshing and nutritious dish that combines the creaminess of avocado with the nutty flavor of quinoa. Packed with protein, healthy fats, and fiber, this salad is not only delicious but also a great option for a light lunch or a side dish for dinner. With its vibrant colors and flavors, it is sure to become a favorite in your household.

Serving: 4 servings
Preparation time: 15 minutes
Ready time: 30 minutes

Ingredients:
- 1 cup quinoa
- 2 cups water
- 2 ripe avocados, diced
- 1 cup cherry tomatoes, halved
- 1/2 cup red onion, finely chopped
- 1/4 cup fresh cilantro, chopped
- 1/4 cup fresh lime juice
- 2 tablespoons olive oil
- Salt and pepper to taste

Instructions:
1. Rinse the quinoa under cold water to remove any bitterness. In a medium saucepan, bring the water to a boil and add the quinoa. Reduce the heat to low, cover, and simmer for about 15 minutes or until the quinoa is tender and the water is absorbed. Remove from heat and let it cool.
2. In a large bowl, combine the cooked quinoa, diced avocados, cherry tomatoes, red onion, and cilantro.
3. In a small bowl, whisk together the lime juice, olive oil, salt, and pepper. Pour the dressing over the quinoa mixture and gently toss to combine.
4. Allow the salad to sit for about 15 minutes to let the flavors meld together.
5. Serve the avocado and quinoa salad chilled or at room temperature. It can be enjoyed as a standalone dish or as a side with grilled chicken or fish.

Nutrition information per Serving: - Calories: 320
- Fat: 18g
- Carbohydrates: 35g
- Fiber: 9g
- Protein: 8g
- Sugar: 2g
- Sodium: 10mg

Note: Nutrition information may vary depending on the specific Ingredients and brands used.

58. Avocado and Bacon Egg Cups

Avocado and Bacon Egg Cups are a delicious and nutritious breakfast option that combines the creaminess of avocado, the smoky flavor of bacon, and the richness of eggs. These individual egg cups are not only easy to make but also packed with protein and healthy fats, making them a perfect way to start your day.

Serving: 4 servings
Preparation time: 10 minutes
Ready time: 25 minutes

Ingredients:
- 2 ripe avocados
- 4 slices of bacon
- 4 large eggs
- Salt and pepper, to taste
- Chopped fresh herbs (such as parsley or chives), for garnish (optional)

Instructions:
1. Preheat your oven to 375°F (190°C). Grease a muffin tin with cooking spray or line it with parchment paper.
2. Cut the avocados in half and remove the pits. Scoop out a small portion of the flesh from each avocado half to create a larger cavity for the egg.
3. Wrap each avocado half with a slice of bacon, making sure to cover the entire circumference. Place the bacon-wrapped avocados in the prepared muffin tin.
4. Crack one egg into each avocado half, being careful not to overflow. Season with salt and pepper to taste.
5. Bake in the preheated oven for about 20-25 minutes or until the eggs are cooked to your desired doneness. If you prefer a runny yolk, check after 15 minutes.
6. Once cooked, remove the avocado and bacon egg cups from the oven and let them cool for a few minutes. Garnish with chopped fresh herbs, if desired.
7. Serve the avocado and bacon egg cups warm and enjoy!

Nutrition information per Serving: - Calories: 250
- Fat: 20g
- Protein: 12g

- Carbohydrates: 6g
- Fiber: 4g
- Sugar: 1g
- Sodium: 250mg

Note: Nutrition information may vary depending on the specific brands and quantities of Ingredients used.

59. Avocado and Chicken Tortilla Soup

Avocado and Chicken Tortilla Soup is a delicious and hearty dish that combines the creaminess of avocado with the savory flavors of chicken and spices. This soup is perfect for a cozy night in or as a starter for a Mexican-inspired meal. With its vibrant colors and rich flavors, it is sure to be a hit with your family and friends.

Serving: 4 servings
Preparation time: 15 minutes
Ready time: 30 minutes

Ingredients:
- 2 boneless, skinless chicken breasts, cooked and shredded
- 1 tablespoon olive oil
- 1 onion, diced
- 3 cloves garlic, minced
- 1 jalapeno pepper, seeded and minced
- 1 teaspoon ground cumin
- 1 teaspoon chili powder
- 4 cups chicken broth
- 1 can diced tomatoes, undrained
- 1 cup corn kernels
- 1 cup black beans, rinsed and drained
- 1 lime, juiced
- Salt and pepper to taste
- 2 avocados, diced
- 1/4 cup fresh cilantro, chopped
- Tortilla chips, for Serving:

Instructions:

1. In a large pot, heat the olive oil over medium heat. Add the diced onion, minced garlic, and jalapeno pepper. Sauté until the onion is translucent and fragrant, about 5 minutes.
2. Add the ground cumin and chili powder to the pot and stir well to coat the vegetables. Cook for an additional 1-2 minutes to toast the spices.
3. Pour in the chicken broth and diced tomatoes with their juice. Bring the mixture to a boil, then reduce the heat and simmer for 10 minutes.
4. Add the shredded chicken, corn kernels, and black beans to the pot. Stir well and continue to simmer for another 10 minutes to allow the flavors to meld together.
5. Stir in the lime juice and season with salt and pepper to taste.
6. To serve, ladle the soup into bowls and top with diced avocado, chopped cilantro, and a handful of tortilla chips for added crunch.
7. Enjoy your Avocado and Chicken Tortilla Soup!

Nutrition information per Serving: - Calories: 350
- Fat: 15g
- Carbohydrates: 30g
- Protein: 25g
- Fiber: 8g

60. Avocado and Lime Cheesecake

Avocado and Lime Cheesecake is a delightful and refreshing dessert that combines the creamy richness of avocado with the tangy zest of lime. This unique twist on a classic cheesecake is sure to impress your guests and leave them wanting more. With its smooth texture and vibrant flavors, this dessert is perfect for any occasion.
Serving: 8 servings
Preparation time: 20 minutes
Ready time: 4 hours (including chilling time)

Ingredients:
- 2 cups graham cracker crumbs
- 1/2 cup unsalted butter, melted
- 3 ripe avocados
- 1 cup granulated sugar

- 1/4 cup fresh lime juice
- 1 tablespoon lime zest
- 1 teaspoon vanilla extract
- 16 ounces cream cheese, softened
- 1 cup heavy cream
- Lime slices, for garnish (optional)

Instructions:
1. In a medium bowl, combine the graham cracker crumbs and melted butter. Mix until the crumbs are evenly coated. Press the mixture into the bottom of a 9-inch springform pan to form the crust. Place the pan in the refrigerator to chill while preparing the filling.
2. In a blender or food processor, combine the avocados, sugar, lime juice, lime zest, and vanilla extract. Blend until smooth and creamy.
3. In a separate bowl, beat the cream cheese until smooth and fluffy. Gradually add the avocado mixture to the cream cheese, beating well after each addition.
4. In another bowl, whip the heavy cream until stiff peaks form. Gently fold the whipped cream into the avocado and cream cheese mixture until well combined.
5. Pour the filling over the chilled crust in the springform pan. Smooth the top with a spatula. Cover the pan with plastic wrap and refrigerate for at least 4 hours, or until set.
6. Once the cheesecake is set, remove it from the refrigerator. Carefully remove the sides of the springform pan. Garnish with lime slices, if desired.
7. Slice and serve chilled. Enjoy the creamy and tangy goodness of this Avocado and Lime Cheesecake!

Nutrition information per Serving: - Calories: 420
- Fat: 30g
- Carbohydrates: 35g
- Protein: 5g
- Fiber: 4g

61. Avocado and Tomato Pita Sandwich

Enjoy the great flavors of avocado and tomato combined together in this delicious pita sandwich.
Serving: 1
Preparation time: 10 minutes
Ready time: 10 minutes

Ingredients:
- 1 whole wheat pita pocket
- 1 avocado, diced
- 1 tomato, diced
- 2 tablespoons of mayonnaise
- Salt and pepper
- 1 teaspoon of lime juice

Instructions:
1. Preheat the oven to 375F.
2. Cut the pita pocket in half and open it up.
3. In a bowl, combine the diced avocado and tomato.
4. Add the mayonnaise and season with salt and pepper, and lime juice.
5. Spread the avocado and tomato mixture onto the pita pocket halves.
6. Bake in the oven for 8 minutes.
7. Enjoy!

Nutrition information: Calories: 458, Total Fat: 24.8g, Saturated Fat: 4.3g, Cholesterol: 12.9mg, Sodium: 428.4mg, Carbohydrates: 47.6g, Dietary Fiber: 9.1g, Sugars: 4.2g, Protein: 11.3g.

62. Avocado and Cucumber Salad

Avocado and Cucumber Salad is a refreshing and healthy dish that combines the creaminess of avocado with the crispness of cucumber. This salad is perfect for hot summer days or as a light side dish for any meal. Packed with vitamins and minerals, it is not only delicious but also nutritious.
Serving: 2 servings
Preparation time: 10 minutes
Ready time: 10 minutes

Ingredients:
- 1 large avocado, diced
- 1 cucumber, peeled and diced
- 1/4 red onion, thinly sliced
- 1/4 cup fresh cilantro, chopped
- 2 tablespoons lime juice
- 1 tablespoon olive oil
- Salt and pepper to taste

Instructions:
1. In a large bowl, combine the diced avocado, cucumber, red onion, and chopped cilantro.
2. In a small bowl, whisk together the lime juice, olive oil, salt, and pepper.
3. Pour the dressing over the avocado and cucumber mixture and gently toss to coat.
4. Serve immediately and enjoy!

Nutrition information:
- Calories: 180
- Fat: 14g
- Carbohydrates: 12g
- Fiber: 7g
- Protein: 2g
- Vitamin C: 20% of the daily recommended intake
- Vitamin K: 26% of the daily recommended intake
- Potassium: 500mg

63. Avocado and Bacon Potato Salad

Avocado and Bacon Potato Salad is a delicious and creamy twist on the classic potato salad. The combination of creamy avocado, crispy bacon, and tender potatoes creates a mouthwatering dish that is perfect for any occasion. Whether you're hosting a barbecue or looking for a tasty side dish, this recipe is sure to impress.
Serving: 4 servings
Preparation time: 15 minutes
Ready time: 30 minutes

Ingredients:
- 4 medium-sized potatoes, peeled and cubed
- 2 ripe avocados, pitted and diced
- 6 slices of bacon, cooked and crumbled
- 1/4 cup red onion, finely chopped
- 1/4 cup fresh cilantro, chopped
- 1/4 cup mayonnaise
- 2 tablespoons lime juice
- Salt and pepper to taste

Instructions:
1. In a large pot, bring water to a boil. Add the cubed potatoes and cook until tender, about 10-12 minutes. Drain and set aside to cool.
2. In a large bowl, combine the diced avocados, crumbled bacon, red onion, and cilantro.
3. In a small bowl, whisk together the mayonnaise and lime juice until well combined. Season with salt and pepper to taste.
4. Add the cooled potatoes to the avocado mixture and gently toss to combine.
5. Pour the mayonnaise-lime dressing over the potato mixture and gently stir until everything is evenly coated.
6. Serve immediately or refrigerate for at least 1 hour to allow the flavors to meld together.
7. Garnish with additional bacon and cilantro, if desired.

Nutrition information per Serving: - Calories: 320
- Fat: 20g
- Carbohydrates: 28g
- Protein: 8g
- Fiber: 6g
- Sugar: 2g
- Sodium: 350mg

Note: Nutrition information may vary depending on the specific Ingredients and brands used.

64. Avocado and Chicken Fajitas

Avocado and chicken fajitas is a great way to spice up your dinner. The combination of flavors will make it a memorable meal for the whole family. This recipe is quick and easy to make and ready in under 30 minutes.

Serving: 4
Preparation Time: 20 minutes
Ready Time: 30 minutes

Ingredients:
- 2 chicken breasts (cut into strips)
- 4 whole wheat tortillas
- 1 tablespoons of olive oil
- 2-3 tablespoons of taco seasoning
- ½ cup of diced onions
- ½ cup of diced bell peppers
- 1 large avocado (diced)
- Chopped cilantro leaves (for garnish)

Instructions:
1. Preheat the oven to 375 degrees Fahrenheit.
2. Place the chicken strips on a baking sheet and season with taco seasoning. Bake in the oven for about 20 minutes.
3. Heat up a pan over medium and add the oil. Sautée the onions, bell peppers and avocado for about 5 minutes, stirring occasionally.
4. Spread the diced Ingredients on each of the tortillas. Add the baked chicken strips.
5. Garnish with cilantro leaves and serve.

Nutrition information: Serving Size: 1 wrap: Calories: 295; Total Fat: 15g; Cholesterol: 43mg; Sodium: 518mg; Total Carbohydrates: 28g; Dietary Fiber: 4g; Protein: 15g.

65. Avocado and Spinach Quiche

Avocado and Spinach Quiche is a delicious and nutritious dish that combines the creaminess of avocado with the freshness of spinach. This quiche is perfect for breakfast, brunch, or even a light dinner. Packed with vitamins and minerals, it is a great way to start your day or refuel after a workout. With its flaky crust and flavorful filling, this quiche is sure to become a favorite in your household.

Serving: 6 servings
Preparation time: 15 minutes
Ready time: 45 minutes

Ingredients:
- 1 pre-made pie crust
- 1 ripe avocado, peeled and pitted
- 2 cups fresh spinach, chopped
- 1 small onion, diced
- 4 large eggs
- 1 cup milk
- 1/2 cup shredded cheddar cheese
- 1/2 teaspoon salt
- 1/4 teaspoon black pepper

Instructions:
1. Preheat your oven to 375°F (190°C).
2. Roll out the pre-made pie crust and press it into a 9-inch pie dish. Trim any excess crust hanging over the edges.
3. In a medium-sized skillet, sauté the diced onion over medium heat until it becomes translucent, about 5 minutes.
4. Add the chopped spinach to the skillet and cook until wilted, about 2-3 minutes. Remove from heat and set aside.
5. In a mixing bowl, mash the ripe avocado until smooth.
6. In a separate bowl, whisk together the eggs, milk, salt, and black pepper.
7. Add the mashed avocado to the egg mixture and whisk until well combined.
8. Spread the sautéed spinach and onion mixture evenly over the bottom of the pie crust.
9. Pour the avocado and egg mixture over the spinach and onion layer.
10. Sprinkle the shredded cheddar cheese on top.
11. Place the quiche in the preheated oven and bake for 30-35 minutes, or until the center is set and the top is golden brown.
12. Remove from the oven and let it cool for a few minutes before slicing and serving.

Nutrition information per Serving: - Calories: 280

- Fat: 18g
- Carbohydrates: 19g
- Protein: 11g
- Fiber: 4g
- Sugar: 3g
- Sodium: 420mg

Note: Nutrition information may vary depending on the brand of Ingredients used.

66. Avocado and Grilled Shrimp Skewers

Avocado and Grilled Shrimp Skewers are a delicious and healthy appetizer or main dish that combines the creaminess of avocado with the smoky flavor of grilled shrimp. These skewers are perfect for summer barbecues or as a light and refreshing meal option. With a simple marinade and quick grilling time, this recipe is easy to make and sure to impress your guests.

Serving: 4 servings
Preparation time: 15 minutes
Ready time: 25 minutes

Ingredients:
- 1 pound of large shrimp, peeled and deveined
- 2 ripe avocados, cut into chunks
- 2 tablespoons of olive oil
- 2 tablespoons of fresh lime juice
- 2 cloves of garlic, minced
- 1 teaspoon of paprika
- 1/2 teaspoon of cayenne pepper (optional, for a spicy kick)
- Salt and pepper to taste
- Wooden skewers, soaked in water for 30 minutes

Instructions:
1. In a bowl, combine the olive oil, lime juice, minced garlic, paprika, cayenne pepper (if using), salt, and pepper. Mix well to create the marinade.
2. Add the shrimp to the marinade and toss to coat evenly. Let the shrimp marinate for 10 minutes.

3. Preheat your grill to medium-high heat.
4. Thread the marinated shrimp and avocado chunks onto the soaked wooden skewers, alternating between shrimp and avocado.
5. Place the skewers on the preheated grill and cook for 2-3 minutes per side, or until the shrimp are pink and opaque.
6. Remove the skewers from the grill and serve hot.

Nutrition information:
- Calories: 250
- Fat: 15g
- Protein: 20g
- Carbohydrates: 10g
- Fiber: 6g
- Sugar: 1g
- Sodium: 300mg

Note: Nutrition information may vary depending on the specific Ingredients and quantities used.

67. Avocado and Tomato Crostini

Avocado and Tomato Crostini is a delicious and refreshing appetizer that combines the creaminess of avocado with the tanginess of tomatoes. This dish is perfect for any occasion, whether it's a casual get-together or a fancy dinner party. The crostini bread adds a satisfying crunch to every bite, making it a crowd-pleaser.

Serving: 4 servings
Preparation time: 10 minutes
Ready time: 15 minutes

Ingredients:
- 1 baguette, sliced into 1/2-inch thick pieces
- 2 ripe avocados
- 1 cup cherry tomatoes, halved
- 1/4 cup red onion, finely chopped
- 2 tablespoons fresh cilantro, chopped
- 1 tablespoon lime juice
- 1 tablespoon olive oil
- Salt and pepper to taste

Instructions:
1. Preheat the oven to 375°F (190°C). Place the baguette slices on a baking sheet and toast them in the oven for about 5 minutes, or until they are golden brown and crispy. Set aside to cool.
2. In a medium-sized bowl, mash the avocados with a fork until they reach your desired consistency. Some prefer a smooth texture, while others like it slightly chunky.
3. Add the cherry tomatoes, red onion, cilantro, lime juice, olive oil, salt, and pepper to the bowl with the mashed avocados. Mix well to combine all the Ingredients.
4. Take each toasted baguette slice and spread a generous amount of the avocado and tomato mixture on top.
5. Arrange the crostini on a serving platter and garnish with additional cilantro, if desired.
6. Serve immediately and enjoy!

Nutrition information per Serving: - Calories: 220
- Fat: 10g
- Carbohydrates: 28g
- Protein: 5g
- Fiber: 4g
- Sugar: 2g
- Sodium: 250mg

Note: Nutrition information may vary depending on the specific Ingredients and brands used.

68. Avocado and Corn Quesadillas

Avocado and corn quesadillas are flavourful, vegetarian quesadillas that require minimal preparation time. The sweetness of the corn combined with the creamy texture of the avocado makes for a great combination of flavours.
Serving: 4
Preparation time: 15 minutes
Ready time: 15 minutes

Ingredients:

- 4 10-inch flour tortillas
- 1 medium avocado, mashed
- 1/4 cup cooked corn
- 1/2 cup shredded Cheddar or monterey jack cheese
- 1 tablespoon vegetable oil

Instructions:
1. Place the flour tortillas on a work surface.
2. Spread a thin layer of mashed avocado on each of the tortillas.
3. Sprinkle the corn and cheese over the avocado.
4. Fold the tortillas in half.
5. Heat the vegetable oil in a large pan over medium heat.
6. Place the quesadillas in the pan and cook until golden brown, about 2-3 minutes per side.
7. Serve immediately.

Nutrition information:
Calories: 348; Total Fat: 17 g; Cholesterol: 19 mg; Sodium: 332 mg; Carbohydrates: 38 g; Fiber: 6 g; Protein: 12 g.

69. Avocado and Goat Cheese Stuffed Burger

Enjoy this delicious twist on the traditional burger with the creamy and savory flavors of avocado and goat cheese.
Serving: 4 burgers
Preparation Time: 10 minutes
Ready Time: 25 minutes

Ingredients:
- 1 large avocado, halved, pitted, peeled, and sliced
- 8 ounces goat cheese, crumbled
- 1 teaspoon fresh lemon juice
- 4 teaspoons mayonnaise
- Salt and pepper to taste
- 1 pound ground beef
- 1 pinch garlic powder
- 4 hamburger buns

Instructions:
1. Preheat an outdoor grill for medium-high heat and lightly oil the grate.
2. In a medium bowl, mix together the avocado, goat cheese, lemon juice, mayonnaise, salt, and pepper.
3. Form the ground beef into four patties.
4. Place a spoonful of the avocado mixture in the center of each patty.
5. Gently fold over the edges of the patty, to form the mixture into a pocket in the center of each patty.
6. Sprinkle the garlic powder over the top of each patty.
7. Grill the patties for about 10 minutes, carefully flipping once.
8. Serve on hamburger buns, with additional avocado and goat cheese, if desired.

Nutrition information:
Calories: 520; Fat: 35g; Cholesterol: 80mg; Sodium: 310mg; Carbohydrates: 17g; Fiber: 4g; Protein: 29g.

70. Avocado and Lime Mousse

Avocado and Lime Mousse is a refreshing and creamy dessert that combines the rich flavors of avocado with the tanginess of lime. This delightful treat is perfect for those who love the combination of sweet and tart flavors. It is also a great way to incorporate healthy fats into your diet, as avocados are packed with nutrients. Whether you serve it as a dessert or a light snack, this Avocado and Lime Mousse is sure to be a crowd-pleaser.

Serving: 4 servings
Preparation time: 15 minutes
Ready time: 2 hours (including chilling time)

Ingredients:
- 2 ripe avocados
- Juice and zest of 2 limes
- 1/4 cup honey or maple syrup
- 1/2 cup coconut milk
- 1 teaspoon vanilla extract
- Pinch of salt
- Fresh mint leaves, for garnish (optional)

Instructions:
1. Cut the avocados in half, remove the pits, and scoop out the flesh into a blender or food processor.
2. Add the lime juice and zest, honey or maple syrup, coconut milk, vanilla extract, and salt to the blender.
3. Blend the mixture until smooth and creamy, scraping down the sides as needed.
4. Taste the mousse and adjust the sweetness or tartness by adding more honey or lime juice, if desired.
5. Transfer the mousse into individual serving glasses or bowls.
6. Cover the glasses or bowls with plastic wrap and refrigerate for at least 2 hours, or until the mousse is set.
7. Before serving, garnish with fresh mint leaves, if desired.
8. Enjoy the Avocado and Lime Mousse chilled.

Nutrition information per Serving: - Calories: 220
- Fat: 15g
- Carbohydrates: 23g
- Fiber: 7g
- Protein: 2g
- Sugar: 14g
- Sodium: 50mg

Note: Nutrition information may vary depending on the specific Ingredients and brands used.

71. Avocado and Bacon Stuffed Mushrooms

Avocado and Bacon Stuffed Mushrooms are a delicious and savory appetizer that combines the creaminess of avocado with the smoky flavor of bacon. These stuffed mushrooms are perfect for parties or as a tasty snack. The combination of flavors and textures will leave your taste buds wanting more!

Serving: 4 servings
Preparation time: 15 minutes
Ready time: 25 minutes

Ingredients:

- 8 large mushrooms
- 1 ripe avocado
- 4 slices of bacon
- 1/4 cup grated Parmesan cheese
- 1/4 cup breadcrumbs
- 1 tablespoon chopped fresh parsley
- 1/2 teaspoon garlic powder
- Salt and pepper to taste

Instructions:
1. Preheat your oven to 375°F (190°C). Line a baking sheet with parchment paper.
2. Remove the stems from the mushrooms and set them aside. Place the mushroom caps on the prepared baking sheet.
3. In a skillet over medium heat, cook the bacon until crispy. Remove the bacon from the skillet and let it cool on a paper towel-lined plate. Once cooled, crumble the bacon into small pieces.
4. In a bowl, mash the avocado until smooth. Add the crumbled bacon, grated Parmesan cheese, breadcrumbs, chopped parsley, garlic powder, salt, and pepper. Mix well to combine.
5. Spoon the avocado and bacon mixture into the mushroom caps, filling each one generously.
6. Finely chop the reserved mushroom stems and sprinkle them over the stuffed mushrooms.
7. Bake the stuffed mushrooms in the preheated oven for 20-25 minutes, or until the mushrooms are tender and the filling is golden brown.
8. Remove from the oven and let them cool for a few minutes before serving.

Nutrition information:
- Calories: 180
- Fat: 12g
- Carbohydrates: 9g
- Protein: 9g
- Fiber: 4g
- Sugar: 1g
- Sodium: 320mg

Note: Nutrition information may vary depending on the specific Ingredients and brands used.

72. Avocado and Black Bean Tacos

Avocado and Black Bean Tacos are a delicious and healthy option for a quick and easy meal. Packed with protein, fiber, and healthy fats, these tacos are not only satisfying but also nutritious. The combination of creamy avocado and hearty black beans creates a flavorful filling that will leave you wanting more. Whether you're a vegetarian or simply looking for a meatless meal option, these tacos are sure to become a favorite in your household.

Serving: 4 tacos
Preparation time: 10 minutes
Ready time: 20 minutes

Ingredients:
- 1 ripe avocado, pitted and mashed
- 1 can black beans, drained and rinsed
- 1 small red onion, diced
- 1 small tomato, diced
- 1 jalapeno pepper, seeded and finely chopped
- 2 tablespoons fresh cilantro, chopped
- 1 tablespoon lime juice
- 1 teaspoon ground cumin
- 1/2 teaspoon chili powder
- Salt and pepper to taste
- 4 small flour tortillas
- Optional toppings: shredded lettuce, diced tomatoes, salsa, sour cream

Instructions:
1. In a medium-sized bowl, combine the mashed avocado, black beans, red onion, tomato, jalapeno pepper, cilantro, lime juice, cumin, chili powder, salt, and pepper. Mix well until all the Ingredients are evenly incorporated.
2. Warm the flour tortillas in a dry skillet over medium heat for about 30 seconds on each side, or until they become pliable.
3. Spoon the avocado and black bean mixture onto each tortilla, dividing it equally among the four tortillas.
4. If desired, top the tacos with shredded lettuce, diced tomatoes, salsa, and sour cream.

5. Fold the tortillas in half, enclosing the filling, and serve immediately.

Nutrition information:
- Calories: 250
- Fat: 10g
- Carbohydrates: 35g
- Fiber: 10g
- Protein: 8g
- Sodium: 300mg

Note: Nutrition information may vary depending on the specific brands and quantities of Ingredients used.

73. Avocado and Tomato Frittata

Avocado and Tomato Frittata is an easy and delicious recipe that will make for a great meal. It's a great way to start the day or just when you feel a little hungry in between meals.
Serving: 4
Preparation time: 10 minutes
Ready time: 25 minutes

Ingredients:
- 8 eggs
- 1 avocado
- 2 tomatoes
- 2 tablespoons olive oil
- 2 cloves minced garlic
- 1/2 teaspoon dried oregano
- Salt and pepper to taste

Instructions:
1. Preheat the oven to 425°F.
2. Grease a 9-inch pie plate with nonstick cooking spray.
3. Slice the avocado and tomatoes into thin slices, and then arrange evenly on the pie plate.
4. Beat the eggs in a medium bowl and season with oregano, salt, and pepper.
5. Pour the egg mixture over the avocado and tomatoes.

6. Place the pie plate in the oven and bake for 18 to 20 minutes, or until the frittata has set and is lightly golden.
7. Remove the frittata from the oven and let it cool before cutting and serving.

Nutrition information: Calories: 230; Fat: 17g; Carbohydrates: 8g; Protein: 12g

74. Avocado and Mango Salad

This fresh and flavorful Avocado and Mango Salad is an easy, delicious side dish, and a perfect way to get a healthy dose of Vitamins and minerals.
Serving: 4
Preparation time: 10 minutes
Ready time: 10 minutes

Ingredients:
- 2 ripe avocados, peeled and diced
- 1 cup diced mango
- ¼ cup finely chopped fresh cilantro
- 2 tablespoons olive oil
- 1 lime, juiced
- ½ teaspoon garlic powder
- ½ teaspoon cumin
- Salt and pepper to taste

Instructions:
1. In a medium bowl, combine the avocado, mango, and cilantro.
2. In a small bowl, whisk together the olive oil, lime juice, garlic powder, cumin, and salt and pepper.
3. Pour the dressing over the avocado and mango mixture and mix gently until all Ingredients are evenly coated.
4. Refrigerate for 10-15 minutes before serving.

Nutrition information:
Calories: 257, Total fat: 21g, Sodium: 10mg, Carbohydrates: 17g, Protein: 2g, Fiber: 6g.

75. Avocado and Spinach Smoothie

This refreshing Avocado and Spinach Smoothie is a perfect way to start your day or enjoy as a healthy snack. Packed with nutrients from avocado and spinach, this smoothie is not only delicious but also incredibly nourishing. The creamy texture of avocado blends perfectly with the vibrant green color of spinach, making it visually appealing as well. Give this smoothie a try and fuel your body with goodness!
Serving: 2 servings
Preparation time: 5 minutes
Ready time: 5 minutes

Ingredients:
- 1 ripe avocado, pitted and peeled
- 2 cups fresh spinach leaves
- 1 banana, peeled
- 1 cup almond milk (or any milk of your choice)
- 1 tablespoon honey or maple syrup (optional, for sweetness)
- Juice of 1/2 lemon
- Ice cubes (optional, for a chilled smoothie)

Instructions:
1. In a blender, combine the avocado, spinach, banana, almond milk, honey or maple syrup (if using), and lemon juice.
2. Blend on high speed until all the Ingredients are well combined and the smoothie is creamy and smooth.
3. If desired, add a few ice cubes and blend again until the smoothie is chilled.
4. Pour the smoothie into glasses and serve immediately.

Nutrition information per Serving: - Calories: 220
- Fat: 12g
- Carbohydrates: 27g
- Fiber: 8g
- Protein: 4g
- Vitamin A: 70% of the Daily Value
- Vitamin C: 40% of the Daily Value

- Calcium: 20% of the Daily Value
- Iron: 10% of the Daily Value

Note: Nutrition information may vary depending on the specific Ingredients and brands used.

76. Avocado and Quinoa Stuffed Zucchini

Avocado and Quinoa Stuffed Zucchini is a delicious and healthy dish that combines the creaminess of avocado with the nutty flavor of quinoa. This recipe is perfect for those looking for a nutritious and filling meal that is also vegetarian and gluten-free. The zucchini boats are stuffed with a flavorful mixture of avocado, quinoa, and other fresh Ingredients, making it a satisfying and wholesome dish.

Serving: 4 servings
Preparation time: 15 minutes
Ready time: 40 minutes

Ingredients:
- 2 large zucchinis
- 1 cup cooked quinoa
- 1 ripe avocado, diced
- 1/2 cup cherry tomatoes, halved
- 1/4 cup red onion, finely chopped
- 1/4 cup fresh cilantro, chopped
- 1 tablespoon lime juice
- 1 tablespoon olive oil
- Salt and pepper to taste

Instructions:
1. Preheat the oven to 375°F (190°C).
2. Cut the zucchinis in half lengthwise and scoop out the seeds to create a hollow space for the stuffing. Place the zucchini halves on a baking sheet lined with parchment paper.
3. In a mixing bowl, combine the cooked quinoa, diced avocado, cherry tomatoes, red onion, cilantro, lime juice, olive oil, salt, and pepper. Mix well until all the Ingredients are evenly incorporated.
4. Spoon the quinoa and avocado mixture into the hollowed-out zucchini halves, dividing it equally among them.

5. Bake the stuffed zucchinis in the preheated oven for about 25-30 minutes, or until the zucchinis are tender and the filling is heated through.
6. Remove from the oven and let them cool for a few minutes before serving.
7. Garnish with additional cilantro, if desired, and serve warm.

Nutrition information per Serving: - Calories: 220
- Fat: 10g
- Carbohydrates: 28g
- Fiber: 8g
- Protein: 6g
- Sodium: 80mg

Note: Nutrition information may vary depending on the specific Ingredients and brands used.

77. Avocado and Bacon Stuffed Jalapenos

This recipe for Avocado and Bacon Stuffed Jalapenos is a flavorful and unique twist on classic stuffed jalapenos. Perfect for the spicy food lover, this delicious and easy to make snack is sure to please!
Serving: 8
Preparation time: 10 minutes
Ready time: 25 minutes

Ingredients:
- 8 jalapenos
- 1/2 ripe avocado
- 4 slices cooked bacon, diced
- 1/4 cup shredded Mexican cheese blend
- 3 tablespoons olive oil
- Salt and pepper to taste

Instructions:
1. Preheat the oven to 400 degrees F.
2. Cut each jalapeno in half lengthwise and then remove and discard the stem, seeds, and inner ribs.

3. In a medium bowl, mash the avocado until smooth then stir in the bacon, cheese, olive oil, salt, and pepper.
4. Divide the avocado mixture evenly among the jalapeno halves and arrange on a baking sheet.
5. Bake for 15 minutes or until the jalapenos are tender and the cheese is melted.
6. Serve warm and enjoy!

Nutrition information:
- Total calories: 217
- Total fat: 16 grams
- Saturated fat: 4.5 grams
- Cholesterol: 13.2 milligrams
- Sodium: 200 milligrams
- Carbohydrates: 11 grams
- Fiber: 4.3 grams
- Protein: 7.2 grams

78. Avocado and Chicken Salad Wrap

This Avocado and Chicken Salad Wrap is a delicious and healthy option for a quick and satisfying meal. Packed with protein from the chicken and healthy fats from the avocado, this wrap is not only tasty but also nutritious. It's perfect for a light lunch or a refreshing dinner option.
Serving: 2 wraps
Preparation time: 15 minutes
Ready time: 15 minutes

Ingredients:
- 2 large tortilla wraps
- 1 cup cooked chicken breast, shredded
- 1 ripe avocado, sliced
- 1/2 cup cherry tomatoes, halved
- 1/4 cup red onion, thinly sliced
- 1/4 cup cucumber, thinly sliced
- 1/4 cup fresh cilantro, chopped
- 2 tablespoons lime juice
- Salt and pepper to taste

Instructions:
1. In a medium-sized bowl, combine the shredded chicken, sliced avocado, cherry tomatoes, red onion, cucumber, and fresh cilantro.
2. Drizzle the lime juice over the mixture and season with salt and pepper to taste. Gently toss everything together until well combined.
3. Lay out the tortilla wraps on a clean surface. Divide the chicken and avocado mixture evenly between the two wraps, placing it in the center of each wrap.
4. Fold the sides of the tortilla wraps over the filling, then roll them up tightly from one end to the other, creating a wrap shape.
5. Cut each wrap in half diagonally to serve.

Nutrition information per Serving: - Calories: 350
- Fat: 15g
- Carbohydrates: 30g
- Protein: 25g
- Fiber: 8g

Note: Nutrition information may vary depending on the specific brands and quantities of Ingredients used.

79. Avocado and Lime Tart

This Avocado and Lime Tart is a refreshing and tangy dessert that combines the creamy richness of avocados with the zesty flavor of lime. It's a perfect treat for those who love the combination of sweet and tart flavors. With a buttery crust and a smooth avocado-lime filling, this tart is sure to impress your guests and satisfy your cravings.

Serving: 8 servings
Preparation time: 20 minutes
Ready time: 2 hours 30 minutes (including chilling time)

Ingredients:
- 1 ½ cups graham cracker crumbs
- 6 tablespoons unsalted butter, melted
- 2 ripe avocados
- 1 cup sweetened condensed milk
- ½ cup fresh lime juice

- 2 teaspoons lime zest
- 1 teaspoon vanilla extract
- Whipped cream, for garnish (optional)
- Lime slices, for garnish (optional)

Instructions:
1. In a medium bowl, combine the graham cracker crumbs and melted butter. Mix until the crumbs are evenly coated with butter.
2. Press the crumb mixture into the bottom and up the sides of a 9-inch tart pan. Use the back of a spoon or a flat-bottomed glass to press the crumbs firmly into place. Place the crust in the refrigerator to chill while you prepare the filling.
3. In a blender or food processor, combine the avocados, sweetened condensed milk, lime juice, lime zest, and vanilla extract. Blend until smooth and creamy.
4. Pour the avocado-lime filling into the chilled crust, spreading it evenly with a spatula.
5. Place the tart in the refrigerator and let it chill for at least 2 hours, or until set.
6. Once the tart is set, remove it from the refrigerator. If desired, garnish with whipped cream and lime slices before serving.
7. Slice the tart into wedges and serve chilled.

Nutrition information per Serving: - Calories: 320
- Fat: 18g
- Carbohydrates: 36g
- Protein: 5g
- Fiber: 4g
- Sugar: 26g
- Sodium: 150mg

Note: Nutrition information may vary depending on the specific Ingredients and brands used.

80. Avocado and Tomato Pasta

Avocado and Tomato Pasta is a delicious and refreshing dish that combines the creaminess of avocado with the tanginess of tomatoes. This pasta is perfect for a quick and easy weeknight dinner or a light lunch. With its vibrant colors and flavors, it is sure to be a hit with both kids and adults alike.

Serving: 4 servings
Preparation time: 10 minutes
Ready time: 20 minutes

Ingredients:
- 8 ounces of pasta (spaghetti or penne)
- 2 ripe avocados
- 1 cup cherry tomatoes, halved
- 2 cloves of garlic, minced
- 1 tablespoon lemon juice
- 2 tablespoons olive oil
- Salt and pepper to taste
- Fresh basil leaves, for garnish

Instructions:
1. Cook the pasta according to the package instructions until al dente. Drain and set aside.
2. While the pasta is cooking, prepare the avocado sauce. Cut the avocados in half, remove the pit, and scoop out the flesh into a blender or food processor.
3. Add the minced garlic, lemon juice, olive oil, salt, and pepper to the blender with the avocado. Blend until smooth and creamy.
4. In a large mixing bowl, combine the cooked pasta, avocado sauce, and cherry tomatoes. Toss gently until the pasta is well coated with the sauce and the tomatoes are evenly distributed.
5. Serve the avocado and tomato pasta in individual bowls or plates. Garnish with fresh basil leaves for added freshness and flavor.
6. Enjoy your creamy and flavorful avocado and tomato pasta!

Nutrition information per Serving: - Calories: 350
- Fat: 18g
- Carbohydrates: 42g
- Protein: 8g
- Fiber: 7g

81. Avocado and Cucumber Roll-Ups

Avocado and Cucumber Roll-Ups are a refreshing and healthy snack or appetizer option. These roll-ups are not only delicious but also packed with nutrients, making them a perfect choice for those looking for a light and nutritious bite. The combination of creamy avocado and crunchy cucumber wrapped in a soft tortilla creates a delightful texture and flavor. Whether you're hosting a party or simply looking for a quick and easy snack, these roll-ups are sure to impress!

Serving: 4 servings
Preparation time: 15 minutes
Ready time: 15 minutes

Ingredients:
- 2 ripe avocados
- 1 large cucumber
- 4 large tortillas (whole wheat or gluten-free, if desired)
- 1/4 cup cream cheese or vegan cream cheese alternative
- 1/4 cup fresh cilantro leaves
- 1/4 cup thinly sliced red onion
- Salt and pepper to taste

Instructions:
1. Start by peeling and slicing the avocados into thin strips. Set aside.
2. Next, wash the cucumber and cut it into thin, long strips. Set aside.
3. Lay out the tortillas on a clean surface and spread a thin layer of cream cheese evenly over each tortilla.
4. Place a few avocado slices, cucumber strips, cilantro leaves, and red onion slices on one end of each tortilla.
5. Season with salt and pepper to taste.
6. Carefully roll up each tortilla tightly, starting from the end with the filling.
7. Once rolled, slice each tortilla into bite-sized pieces, about 1 inch thick.
8. Serve the avocado and cucumber roll-ups immediately or refrigerate until ready to serve.

Nutrition information:
- Serving size: 1 roll-up
- Calories: 150

- Total fat: 8g
- Saturated fat: 2g
- Cholesterol: 5mg
- Sodium: 200mg
- Total carbohydrates: 18g
- Dietary fiber: 5g
- Sugars: 2g
- Protein: 4g

Note: Nutrition information may vary depending on the specific brands and quantities of Ingredients used.

82. Avocado and Black Bean Burgers

Avocado and Black Bean Burgers are a delicious and healthy alternative to traditional meat burgers. Packed with protein and fiber, these burgers are not only tasty but also nutritious. The combination of creamy avocado and hearty black beans creates a satisfying and flavorful patty that will leave you wanting more. Whether you're a vegetarian or simply looking to incorporate more plant-based meals into your diet, these burgers are sure to be a hit!

Serving: 4 burgers
Preparation time: 15 minutes
Ready time: 30 minutes

Ingredients:
- 1 ripe avocado, mashed
- 1 can (15 ounces) black beans, drained and rinsed
- 1/2 cup breadcrumbs
- 1/4 cup red onion, finely chopped
- 2 cloves garlic, minced
- 1/4 cup cilantro, chopped
- 1 teaspoon cumin
- 1/2 teaspoon paprika
- Salt and pepper to taste
- 4 burger buns
- Optional toppings: lettuce, tomato, onion, pickles, etc.

Instructions:

1. In a large mixing bowl, combine the mashed avocado, black beans, breadcrumbs, red onion, garlic, cilantro, cumin, paprika, salt, and pepper. Mix well until all the Ingredients are evenly incorporated.
2. Form the mixture into 4 equal-sized patties, about 1/2 inch thick. If the mixture is too wet, add more breadcrumbs to help bind it together.
3. Heat a non-stick skillet or grill pan over medium heat. Lightly grease the pan with cooking spray or a small amount of oil.
4. Cook the avocado and black bean patties for about 5-6 minutes on each side, or until they are golden brown and heated through.
5. While the patties are cooking, lightly toast the burger buns if desired.
6. Assemble the burgers by placing a patty on each bun and adding your favorite toppings such as lettuce, tomato, onion, and pickles.
7. Serve the avocado and black bean burgers immediately and enjoy!

Nutrition information (per serving):
- Calories: 320
- Total fat: 9g
- Saturated fat: 1g
- Cholesterol: 0mg
- Sodium: 480mg
- Total carbohydrates: 51g
- Dietary fiber: 12g
- Sugars: 4g
- Protein: 13g

Note: Nutrition information may vary depending on the specific Ingredients and brands used.

83. Avocado and Goat Cheese Stuffed Peppers

Avocado and Goat Cheese Stuffed Peppers are a delicious and healthy appetizer or side dish that is sure to impress your guests. The combination of creamy avocado and tangy goat cheese creates a flavorful filling that perfectly complements the sweetness of the roasted peppers. This recipe is easy to make and can be customized to suit your taste preferences.

Serving: 4 servings
Preparation time: 15 minutes
Ready time: 30 minutes

Ingredients:
- 4 large bell peppers (any color)
- 2 ripe avocados
- 4 ounces goat cheese
- 1/4 cup diced red onion
- 1/4 cup chopped fresh cilantro
- 1 tablespoon lime juice
- Salt and pepper to taste

Instructions:
1. Preheat your oven to 400°F (200°C). Line a baking sheet with parchment paper.
2. Cut the bell peppers in half lengthwise and remove the seeds and membranes. Place the pepper halves on the prepared baking sheet, cut side up.
3. In a medium bowl, mash the avocados with a fork until smooth. Add the goat cheese, red onion, cilantro, lime juice, salt, and pepper. Stir until well combined.
4. Spoon the avocado and goat cheese mixture into each pepper half, filling them evenly.
5. Bake the stuffed peppers in the preheated oven for 20-25 minutes, or until the peppers are tender and slightly charred.
6. Remove from the oven and let them cool for a few minutes before serving.

Nutrition information per Serving: - Calories: 180
- Fat: 13g
- Carbohydrates: 12g
- Fiber: 6g
- Protein: 6g
- Sodium: 150mg

84. Avocado and Lime Sorbet

Avocado and Lime Sorbet is a refreshing and tangy dessert that combines the creamy texture of avocado with the zesty flavor of lime. This sorbet is not only delicious but also a healthy treat, as avocados are packed with nutrients and good fats. It's the perfect dessert to cool down on a hot summer day or to enjoy after a spicy meal.

Serving: 4 servings
Preparation time: 10 minutes
Ready time: 4 hours (including freezing time)

Ingredients:
- 2 ripe avocados
- Juice and zest of 2 limes
- 1/2 cup of granulated sugar
- 1 cup of water

Instructions:
1. Cut the avocados in half, remove the pits, and scoop out the flesh into a blender or food processor.
2. Add the lime juice and zest, sugar, and water to the blender.
3. Blend the mixture until smooth and creamy.
4. Taste the mixture and adjust the sweetness by adding more sugar if desired.
5. Pour the mixture into an ice cream maker and churn according to the manufacturer's instructions until it reaches a sorbet-like consistency. This usually takes about 20-30 minutes.
6. If you don't have an ice cream maker, pour the mixture into a shallow dish and place it in the freezer.
7. Every 30 minutes, take the dish out and use a fork to scrape and mix the partially frozen mixture. Repeat this process for about 3-4 hours, or until the sorbet is firm and scoopable.
8. Once the sorbet is ready, transfer it to an airtight container and store it in the freezer until serving.

Nutrition information per Serving: - Calories: 180
- Fat: 10g
- Carbohydrates: 23g
- Fiber: 5g
- Protein: 2g
- Sugar: 16g
- Sodium: 5mg

Note: Nutrition information may vary depending on the size and ripeness of the avocados used.

85. Avocado and Bacon Mac and Cheese

Avocado and Bacon Mac and Cheese is a delicious twist on the classic comfort food. Creamy avocado and crispy bacon add a burst of flavor to this cheesy pasta dish. It's the perfect combination of creamy, savory, and indulgent. Whether you're looking for a quick weeknight dinner or a crowd-pleasing dish for a gathering, this recipe is sure to satisfy your cravings.

Serving: 4 servings
Preparation time: 15 minutes
Ready time: 30 minutes

Ingredients:
- 8 ounces elbow macaroni
- 4 slices bacon, cooked and crumbled
- 1 ripe avocado, peeled and pitted
- 1 cup shredded cheddar cheese
- 1/2 cup shredded mozzarella cheese
- 1/2 cup milk
- 2 tablespoons butter
- 2 tablespoons all-purpose flour
- 1/2 teaspoon garlic powder
- 1/2 teaspoon onion powder
- Salt and pepper to taste

Instructions:
1. Cook the elbow macaroni according to the package instructions. Drain and set aside.
2. In a large skillet, melt the butter over medium heat. Add the flour and whisk until smooth, cooking for about 1 minute.
3. Slowly pour in the milk while whisking continuously. Cook until the mixture thickens, about 2-3 minutes.
4. Add the shredded cheddar cheese and mozzarella cheese to the skillet, stirring until melted and smooth.
5. Mash the avocado in a separate bowl until smooth. Add the mashed avocado, garlic powder, onion powder, salt, and pepper to the cheese sauce. Stir until well combined.

6. Add the cooked macaroni and crumbled bacon to the skillet, stirring until the pasta is evenly coated with the cheese sauce.
7. Cook for an additional 2-3 minutes, or until heated through.
8. Serve the avocado and bacon mac and cheese hot, garnished with additional crumbled bacon if desired.

Nutrition information per Serving: - Calories: 450
- Fat: 25g
- Carbohydrates: 38g
- Protein: 18g
- Fiber: 4g

86. Avocado and Chicken Lettuce Cups

Avocado and Chicken Lettuce Cups are a delicious and healthy option for a light meal or appetizer. These refreshing lettuce cups are filled with creamy avocado, tender chicken, and a burst of flavors from various Ingredients. They are not only easy to make but also packed with nutrients, making them a perfect choice for those looking for a nutritious and satisfying dish.
Serving: 4 servings
Preparation time: 15 minutes
Ready time: 15 minutes

Ingredients:
- 2 cups cooked chicken breast, shredded
- 2 ripe avocados, diced
- 1/2 cup cherry tomatoes, halved
- 1/4 cup red onion, finely chopped
- 1/4 cup fresh cilantro, chopped
- 2 tablespoons lime juice
- 1 tablespoon olive oil
- Salt and pepper to taste
- 8 large lettuce leaves (such as butter lettuce or romaine)

Instructions:
1. In a large bowl, combine the shredded chicken, diced avocados, cherry tomatoes, red onion, and cilantro.

2. In a small bowl, whisk together the lime juice, olive oil, salt, and pepper.
3. Pour the dressing over the chicken and avocado mixture. Gently toss until well combined.
4. Take a lettuce leaf and spoon a generous amount of the avocado and chicken mixture onto it.
5. Repeat with the remaining lettuce leaves and filling.
6. Serve immediately and enjoy!

Nutrition information per Serving: - Calories: 250
- Fat: 15g
- Carbohydrates: 10g
- Protein: 20g
- Fiber: 6g
- Sugar: 2g
- Sodium: 150mg

Note: Nutrition information may vary depending on the specific Ingredients and brands used.

87. Avocado and Strawberry Salad

Avocado and Strawberry Salad is a refreshing and nutritious dish that combines the creaminess of avocado with the sweetness of strawberries. This salad is perfect for a light lunch or as a side dish for a summer barbecue. Packed with vitamins and antioxidants, it is not only delicious but also good for your health.

Serving: 2 servings
Preparation time: 10 minutes
Ready time: 10 minutes

Ingredients:
- 1 ripe avocado, peeled, pitted, and sliced
- 1 cup fresh strawberries, hulled and sliced
- 2 cups mixed salad greens
- 1/4 cup crumbled feta cheese
- 2 tablespoons chopped fresh mint leaves
- 2 tablespoons chopped walnuts

For the dressing:

- 2 tablespoons extra virgin olive oil
- 1 tablespoon balsamic vinegar
- 1 teaspoon honey
- Salt and pepper to taste

Instructions:
1. In a large salad bowl, combine the mixed salad greens, avocado slices, and strawberry slices.
2. In a small bowl, whisk together the olive oil, balsamic vinegar, honey, salt, and pepper to make the dressing.
3. Drizzle the dressing over the salad and gently toss to coat all the Ingredients.
4. Sprinkle the crumbled feta cheese, chopped mint leaves, and chopped walnuts over the salad.
5. Serve immediately and enjoy!

Nutrition information per Serving: - Calories: 250
- Fat: 20g
- Carbohydrates: 15g
- Fiber: 7g
- Protein: 5g
- Vitamin C: 60% of the daily recommended intake
- Vitamin A: 15% of the daily recommended intake
- Calcium: 10% of the daily recommended intake
- Iron: 8% of the daily recommended intake

Note: Nutrition information may vary depending on the specific brands of Ingredients used.

88. Avocado and Spinach Pesto Pasta

Avocado and Spinach Pesto Pasta is a delicious and nutritious dish that combines the creaminess of avocado with the freshness of spinach. This pasta dish is not only easy to make but also packed with vitamins and minerals, making it a perfect choice for a quick and healthy meal.
Serving: 4 servings
Preparation time: 15 minutes
Ready time: 25 minutes

Ingredients:
- 8 ounces of whole wheat pasta
- 1 ripe avocado
- 2 cups of fresh spinach leaves
- 1/4 cup of fresh basil leaves
- 2 cloves of garlic, minced
- 1/4 cup of pine nuts
- 1/4 cup of grated Parmesan cheese
- 2 tablespoons of lemon juice
- 1/4 cup of extra virgin olive oil
- Salt and pepper to taste

Instructions:
1. Cook the whole wheat pasta according to the package instructions until al dente. Drain and set aside.
2. In a food processor or blender, combine the ripe avocado, fresh spinach leaves, basil leaves, minced garlic, pine nuts, grated Parmesan cheese, lemon juice, and extra virgin olive oil. Blend until smooth and creamy.
3. Season the avocado and spinach pesto with salt and pepper to taste.
4. In a large mixing bowl, combine the cooked pasta and the avocado and spinach pesto. Toss until the pasta is evenly coated with the pesto sauce.
5. Serve the avocado and spinach pesto pasta warm or at room temperature. You can garnish it with additional grated Parmesan cheese and a sprinkle of pine nuts, if desired.

Nutrition information per Serving: - Calories: 380
- Fat: 20g
- Carbohydrates: 40g
- Fiber: 8g
- Protein: 12g
- Sodium: 150mg

Note: Nutrition information may vary depending on the specific Ingredients and brands used.

89. Avocado and Quinoa Stuffed Tomatoes

Avocado and Quinoa Stuffed Tomatoes are a delicious and healthy dish that combines the creaminess of avocado with the nuttiness of quinoa. This recipe is perfect for a light lunch or as a side dish for dinner. The combination of flavors and textures will leave you satisfied and nourished.

Serving: 4 servings
Preparation time: 15 minutes
Ready time: 30 minutes

Ingredients:
- 4 large tomatoes
- 1 cup cooked quinoa
- 1 ripe avocado, diced
- 1/4 cup red onion, finely chopped
- 1/4 cup fresh cilantro, chopped
- 1 tablespoon lime juice
- 1 tablespoon olive oil
- Salt and pepper to taste

Instructions:
1. Preheat the oven to 350°F (175°C).
2. Cut off the tops of the tomatoes and scoop out the seeds and pulp using a spoon. Set aside.
3. In a mixing bowl, combine the cooked quinoa, diced avocado, red onion, cilantro, lime juice, olive oil, salt, and pepper. Mix well until all the Ingredients are evenly distributed.
4. Stuff each tomato with the quinoa and avocado mixture, pressing it down gently to fill the cavity.
5. Place the stuffed tomatoes on a baking sheet and bake in the preheated oven for 15-20 minutes, or until the tomatoes are slightly softened.
6. Remove from the oven and let them cool for a few minutes before serving.

Nutrition information per Serving: - Calories: 180
- Fat: 10g
- Carbohydrates: 20g
- Fiber: 6g
- Protein: 4g
- Sodium: 80mg

Note: Nutrition information may vary depending on the size of the tomatoes and the specific brands of Ingredients used.

90. Avocado and Bacon Tacos

Avocado and Bacon Tacos are a delicious and satisfying meal option that combines the creaminess of avocado with the smoky flavor of bacon. These tacos are perfect for breakfast, lunch, or dinner and can be customized with your favorite toppings. Get ready to indulge in this mouthwatering treat!

Serving: 4 tacos
Preparation time: 10 minutes
Ready time: 20 minutes

Ingredients:
- 4 small tortillas (corn or flour)
- 2 ripe avocados
- 6 slices of bacon
- 1 small red onion, thinly sliced
- 1 jalapeno pepper, seeded and diced
- 1 lime, juiced
- Salt and pepper to taste
- Optional toppings: shredded cheese, salsa, sour cream, cilantro

Instructions:
1. Preheat your oven to 400°F (200°C). Place the bacon slices on a baking sheet lined with parchment paper and bake for about 15 minutes or until crispy. Remove from the oven and set aside to cool.
2. While the bacon is cooking, cut the avocados in half, remove the pits, and scoop out the flesh into a bowl. Mash the avocado with a fork until it reaches your desired consistency. Add the lime juice, salt, and pepper, and mix well.
3. Warm the tortillas in a dry skillet over medium heat for about 30 seconds on each side, or until they become pliable. Remove from the skillet and set aside.
4. Once the bacon has cooled, crumble it into small pieces.

5. To assemble the tacos, spread a generous amount of the mashed avocado onto each tortilla. Top with crumbled bacon, sliced red onion, and diced jalapeno. Add any optional toppings you desire.
6. Serve the avocado and bacon tacos immediately and enjoy!

Nutrition information (per serving):
- Calories: 320
- Fat: 20g
- Carbohydrates: 25g
- Protein: 10g
- Fiber: 8g
- Sugar: 2g
- Sodium: 450mg

Note: Nutrition information may vary depending on the type and amount of toppings used.

91. Avocado and Tomato Salsa

Avocado and Tomato Salsa is a refreshing and healthy dish that combines the creaminess of avocado with the tanginess of tomatoes. This salsa is perfect as a dip, topping for tacos or grilled meats, or even as a side dish. It is quick and easy to make, and the vibrant colors make it visually appealing as well.

Serving: 4 servings
Preparation time: 10 minutes
Ready time: 10 minutes

Ingredients:
- 2 ripe avocados, diced
- 2 medium tomatoes, diced
- 1 small red onion, finely chopped
- 1 jalapeno pepper, seeds removed and finely chopped
- 1/4 cup fresh cilantro, chopped
- Juice of 1 lime
- Salt and pepper to taste

Instructions:

1. In a medium-sized bowl, combine the diced avocados, tomatoes, red onion, jalapeno pepper, and cilantro.
2. Squeeze the lime juice over the mixture and gently toss to combine.
3. Season with salt and pepper to taste.
4. Serve immediately or refrigerate for up to 1 hour to allow the flavors to meld together.
5. Serve as a dip with tortilla chips, as a topping for tacos or grilled meats, or as a side dish.

Nutrition information per Serving: - Calories: 120
- Fat: 9g
- Carbohydrates: 10g
- Fiber: 6g
- Protein: 2g
- Vitamin C: 20% of the daily recommended intake
- Vitamin A: 10% of the daily recommended intake
- Calcium: 2% of the daily recommended intake
- Iron: 4% of the daily recommended intake

92. Avocado and Corn Fritters

Avocado and Corn Fritters are a delicious and nutritious snack or side dish that can be enjoyed by everyone. These fritters are packed with the goodness of avocados and sweet corn, making them a perfect choice for a quick and easy meal. The crispy exterior and creamy interior of these fritters will leave you craving for more.
Serving: 4 servings
Preparation time: 15 minutes
Ready time: 25 minutes

Ingredients:
- 2 ripe avocados, peeled and pitted
- 1 cup sweet corn kernels (fresh or frozen)
- 1/2 cup all-purpose flour
- 1/4 cup cornmeal
- 1/4 cup chopped fresh cilantro
- 1/4 cup diced red onion
- 1 teaspoon baking powder

- 1/2 teaspoon salt
- 1/4 teaspoon black pepper
- 1/4 teaspoon cayenne pepper (optional)
- 2 large eggs, beaten
- Vegetable oil, for frying

Instructions:
1. In a large bowl, mash the avocados until smooth. Add the sweet corn, flour, cornmeal, cilantro, red onion, baking powder, salt, black pepper, and cayenne pepper (if using). Mix well to combine.
2. Add the beaten eggs to the avocado mixture and stir until everything is well incorporated.
3. Heat vegetable oil in a large skillet over medium heat.
4. Drop spoonfuls of the avocado and corn mixture into the hot oil, flattening them slightly with the back of the spoon. Cook for about 3-4 minutes on each side, or until golden brown and crispy.
5. Remove the fritters from the skillet and place them on a paper towel-lined plate to drain excess oil.
6. Serve the avocado and corn fritters warm with your favorite dipping sauce or as a side dish to complement your main course.

Nutrition information:
- Calories: 220
- Fat: 12g
- Carbohydrates: 24g
- Protein: 6g
- Fiber: 5g
- Sugar: 2g
- Sodium: 320mg

Note: Nutrition information may vary depending on the specific Ingredients and quantities used.

93. Avocado and Goat Cheese Stuffed Chicken

Avocado and Goat Cheese Stuffed Chicken is a delicious and healthy dish that combines the creaminess of avocado and the tanginess of goat cheese. This recipe is perfect for a special dinner or a weeknight meal that will impress your family and friends. The chicken breasts are stuffed

with a flavorful mixture of avocado, goat cheese, and herbs, then baked to perfection. With its creamy filling and juicy chicken, this dish is sure to become a favorite in your household.
Serving: 4 servings
Preparation time: 15 minutes
Ready time: 35 minutes

Ingredients:
- 4 boneless, skinless chicken breasts
- 1 ripe avocado, pitted and mashed
- 4 ounces goat cheese, crumbled
- 2 tablespoons fresh basil, chopped
- 2 tablespoons fresh parsley, chopped
- 1 teaspoon garlic powder
- 1/2 teaspoon salt
- 1/4 teaspoon black pepper
- 1 tablespoon olive oil

Instructions:
1. Preheat your oven to 375°F (190°C).
2. In a medium bowl, combine the mashed avocado, goat cheese, basil, parsley, garlic powder, salt, and black pepper. Mix well until all the Ingredients are evenly incorporated.
3. Using a sharp knife, make a horizontal slit in each chicken breast to create a pocket for the stuffing. Be careful not to cut all the way through.
4. Stuff each chicken breast with the avocado and goat cheese mixture, dividing it equally among the four breasts.
5. Heat the olive oil in a large oven-safe skillet over medium-high heat. Once hot, add the stuffed chicken breasts to the skillet and sear them for about 2 minutes on each side, or until they are golden brown.
6. Transfer the skillet to the preheated oven and bake the chicken for 20-25 minutes, or until the internal temperature reaches 165°F (74°C) and the chicken is cooked through.
7. Remove the skillet from the oven and let the chicken rest for a few minutes before serving.
8. Serve the Avocado and Goat Cheese Stuffed Chicken with your favorite side dishes, such as roasted vegetables or a fresh salad.

Nutrition information per Serving: - Calories: 320
- Fat: 18g

- Carbohydrates: 4g
- Protein: 35g
- Fiber: 2g

94. Avocado and Lime Popsicles

Avocado and Lime Popsicles are a refreshing and healthy treat perfect for hot summer days. These creamy and tangy popsicles are made with ripe avocados and zesty lime juice, creating a delightful combination of flavors. Whether you're looking for a guilt-free dessert or a fun snack, these popsicles are sure to satisfy your cravings.
Serving: Makes 6 popsicles
Preparation time: 10 minutes
Ready time: 4 hours (including freezing time)

Ingredients:
- 2 ripe avocados
- Juice of 2 limes
- 1/4 cup honey or maple syrup (adjust to taste)
- 1 cup coconut milk
- 1/2 teaspoon vanilla extract

Instructions:
1. Cut the avocados in half, remove the pits, and scoop out the flesh into a blender or food processor.
2. Add the lime juice, honey or maple syrup, coconut milk, and vanilla extract to the blender.
3. Blend the mixture until smooth and creamy.
4. Taste the mixture and adjust the sweetness by adding more honey or maple syrup if desired.
5. Pour the mixture into popsicle molds, leaving a little space at the top for expansion during freezing.
6. Insert popsicle sticks into each mold.
7. Place the molds in the freezer and let them freeze for at least 4 hours or until completely solid.
8. Once the popsicles are frozen, remove them from the molds by running them under warm water for a few seconds.
9. Serve immediately and enjoy!

Nutrition information (per serving):
- Calories: 180
- Fat: 14g
- Carbohydrates: 15g
- Fiber: 5g
- Protein: 2g
- Sugar: 9g
- Sodium: 10mg

Note: Nutrition information may vary depending on the size of the avocados and the brand of coconut milk used.

95. Avocado and Tomato Tartines

Avocado and Tomato Tartines are a delicious and healthy snack option. The briny, flavorful Ingredients bring out the best in one another, creating a unique yet simple toast that's perfect for lunch or as an afternoon snack. This recipe is easy to make and takes only a few minutes to prepare.

Serving: Serves 2
Preparation time: 5 minutes
Ready time: 10 minutes

Ingredients:
- 2 slices of whole wheat bread
- 2 Tbsp of olive oil
- 1 avocado, thinly sliced
- 4 grape tomatoes, halved
- 1 shallot, finely diced
- 1 Tbsp of feta cheese, crumbled
- Salt and pepper, to taste

Instructions:
1. Preheat the oven to 350F.
2. Arrange the bread slices on a lined baking sheet.
3. Drizzle with olive oil.
4. Top with avocado slices, grape tomatoes, and shallot.
5. Sprinkle with feta cheese and season with salt and pepper.

6. Bake for 8-10 minutes, or until the bread is toasted and the cheese is melted.
7. Serve warm.

Nutrition information:
Calories: 234
Total Fat: 16g
Saturated Fat: 3g
Cholesterol: 6mg
Sodium: 175mg
Carbohydrates: 17g
Fiber: 5g
Sugar: 2g
Protein: 5g

96. Avocado and Black Bean Stuffed Sweet Potatoes

Avocado and Black Bean Stuffed Sweet Potatoes are a delicious and nutritious meal that combines the creaminess of avocado, the heartiness of black beans, and the sweetness of sweet potatoes. This dish is not only packed with flavor but also provides a good source of fiber, protein, and healthy fats. It's a perfect option for a quick and satisfying lunch or dinner.
Serving: 4 servings
Preparation time: 10 minutes
Ready time: 1 hour

Ingredients:
- 4 medium-sized sweet potatoes
- 1 can (15 ounces) black beans, rinsed and drained
- 2 ripe avocados, peeled and diced
- 1 small red onion, finely chopped
- 1 small red bell pepper, finely chopped
- 1 jalapeno pepper, seeds removed and finely chopped (optional)
- 1/4 cup fresh cilantro, chopped
- Juice of 1 lime
- 1 teaspoon ground cumin
- 1/2 teaspoon chili powder

- Salt and pepper to taste

Instructions:
1. Preheat the oven to 400°F (200°C).
2. Wash the sweet potatoes thoroughly and prick them with a fork all over. Place them on a baking sheet and bake for about 45-60 minutes, or until they are tender and easily pierced with a fork.
3. While the sweet potatoes are baking, prepare the avocado and black bean filling. In a large bowl, combine the black beans, diced avocados, red onion, red bell pepper, jalapeno pepper (if using), and cilantro.
4. In a small bowl, whisk together the lime juice, ground cumin, chili powder, salt, and pepper. Pour the dressing over the avocado and black bean mixture and gently toss to combine.
5. Once the sweet potatoes are cooked, remove them from the oven and let them cool slightly. Cut a slit lengthwise in each sweet potato, being careful not to cut all the way through.
6. Stuff each sweet potato with the avocado and black bean mixture, dividing it evenly among them.
7. Serve the stuffed sweet potatoes warm, garnished with additional cilantro if desired.

Nutrition information per Serving: - Calories: 320
- Fat: 12g
- Carbohydrates: 48g
- Fiber: 14g
- Protein: 10g

97. Avocado and Cucumber Gazpacho

Avocado and Cucumber Gazpacho is a cool and refreshing summer soup made with tangy cucumber, creamy avocado, and zippy tomatoes. It's a great way to enjoy some seasonal produce.
Serving: Makes 4 servings
Preparation time: 15 minutes
Ready time: 15 minutes

Ingredients:
- 2 ripe avocados, diced

- 1 large cucumber, diced
- 2 tomatoes, diced
- 1/4 cup chopped red onions
- 3 tablespoons freshly squeezed lime juice
- 1 tablespoon extra virgin olive oil
- Salt and pepper to taste

Instructions:
1. In a medium bowl, combine avocados, cucumbers, tomatoes, and red onions.
2. In a separate small bowl, whisk together lime juice, olive oil, salt, and pepper.
3. Pour the dressing over the vegetables and toss to combine.
4. Serve chilled.

Nutrition information (per serving): Calories: 209 Carbs: 17g Protein: 2g Fat: 16g Fiber: 7g

98. Avocado and Bacon Breakfast Pizza

Start your day off right with this delicious and satisfying Avocado and Bacon Breakfast Pizza. Packed with protein and healthy fats, this pizza is a perfect combination of flavors that will keep you energized throughout the morning. Whether you're hosting a brunch or simply looking for a quick and easy breakfast option, this recipe is sure to impress.
Serving: 4 servings
Preparation time: 10 minutes
Ready time: 20 minutes

Ingredients:
- 1 pre-made pizza dough
- 4 slices of bacon, cooked and crumbled
- 1 ripe avocado, sliced
- 4 large eggs
- 1 cup shredded mozzarella cheese
- Salt and pepper to taste
- Fresh cilantro or parsley for garnish (optional)

Instructions:
1. Preheat your oven to the temperature specified on the pizza dough package.
2. Roll out the pizza dough on a lightly floured surface to your desired thickness.
3. Transfer the rolled-out dough onto a baking sheet or pizza stone.
4. Sprinkle the shredded mozzarella cheese evenly over the dough.
5. Arrange the sliced avocado and crumbled bacon on top of the cheese.
6. Create four small wells in the toppings, evenly spaced apart.
7. Carefully crack an egg into each well, making sure not to break the yolk.
8. Season the eggs with salt and pepper to taste.
9. Place the baking sheet or pizza stone in the preheated oven and bake for about 15-20 minutes, or until the crust is golden brown and the eggs are cooked to your desired level of doneness.
10. Remove from the oven and let it cool for a few minutes.
11. Garnish with fresh cilantro or parsley, if desired.
12. Slice the pizza into wedges and serve hot.

Nutrition information per Serving: - Calories: 380
- Fat: 22g
- Carbohydrates: 28g
- Protein: 18g
- Fiber: 4g

Note: Nutrition information may vary depending on the specific brands and quantities of Ingredients used.

99. Avocado and Chicken Fajita Salad

This Avocado and Chicken Fajita Salad is a delicious and healthy option for a light lunch or dinner. Packed with fresh Ingredients and bursting with flavors, this salad is sure to satisfy your taste buds. The combination of creamy avocado, tender chicken, and colorful vegetables makes it a perfect choice for a quick and easy meal.

Serving: 2 servings
Preparation time: 15 minutes
Ready time: 20 minutes

Ingredients:
- 2 boneless, skinless chicken breasts
- 1 tablespoon olive oil
- 1 red bell pepper, sliced
- 1 green bell pepper, sliced
- 1 yellow bell pepper, sliced
- 1 red onion, sliced
- 1 teaspoon chili powder
- 1 teaspoon cumin
- 1 teaspoon paprika
- Salt and pepper to taste
- 2 avocados, sliced
- 4 cups mixed salad greens
- 1/4 cup cilantro leaves, chopped
- Juice of 1 lime

Instructions:
1. Preheat your grill or stovetop grill pan over medium-high heat.
2. Season the chicken breasts with salt, pepper, chili powder, cumin, and paprika.
3. Drizzle olive oil over the chicken breasts and rub the spices into the meat.
4. Grill the chicken for about 6-8 minutes per side, or until cooked through. Remove from heat and let it rest for a few minutes before slicing.
5. In the meantime, heat a tablespoon of olive oil in a large skillet over medium heat.
6. Add the sliced bell peppers and onion to the skillet and sauté until they are tender and slightly charred, about 5-7 minutes. Season with salt and pepper to taste.
7. In a large salad bowl, combine the mixed salad greens, sliced avocado, and cilantro leaves.
8. Add the grilled chicken slices and sautéed bell peppers and onion to the salad bowl.
9. Squeeze the juice of one lime over the salad and toss gently to combine all the Ingredients.
10. Serve the Avocado and Chicken Fajita Salad immediately and enjoy!

Nutrition information:
- Calories: 380

- Fat: 22g
- Carbohydrates: 18g
- Protein: 30g
- Fiber: 10g

100. Avocado and Lime Margarita

Avocado and Lime Margarita is a refreshing and creamy twist on the classic margarita. The combination of creamy avocado and tangy lime creates a unique and delicious flavor that will surely impress your guests. This cocktail is perfect for summer gatherings or simply for enjoying a relaxing evening at home.
Serving: 2 servings
Preparation time: 10 minutes
Ready time: 10 minutes

Ingredients:
- 1 ripe avocado
- Juice of 2 limes
- 4 ounces tequila
- 2 ounces triple sec
- 1 tablespoon agave syrup (optional, for sweetness)
- Ice cubes
- Lime wedges, for garnish
- Salt, for rimming the glasses (optional)

Instructions:
1. Cut the avocado in half, remove the pit, and scoop out the flesh into a blender or food processor.
2. Add the lime juice, tequila, triple sec, and agave syrup (if using) to the blender.
3. Blend until smooth and creamy.
4. If desired, rim the glasses with salt by running a lime wedge around the rim and dipping it into a plate of salt.
5. Fill the glasses with ice cubes.
6. Pour the avocado and lime mixture over the ice.
7. Garnish with lime wedges.
8. Stir gently and serve immediately.

Nutrition information per Serving: - Calories: 250
- Fat: 10g
- Carbohydrates: 20g
- Fiber: 8g
- Protein: 2g
- Sugar: 8g
- Sodium: 10mg

Note: Nutrition information may vary depending on the specific Ingredients and brands used.

CONCLUSION

The cookbook "Guac Your World: 100 Recipes for Avocado Lovers" offers a plethora of delicious, nutritious, and creative recipes that showcase the incredible versatility and potential of the beloved avocado. From savory and spicy dishes to creamy smoothies and desserts, the recipes in this cookbook provide something for everyone. Avocados provide essential nutrients such as potassium, fiber, and vitamins that are important for maintaining a healthy diet; by incorporating them into your daily meals, you can improve your overall wellbeing.

Creating dishes with avocados has been a passion for many home cooks over the years, and "Guac Your World" provides them with a wealth of ideas and inspiration. This cookbook can help you feel confident in the kitchen, and it can give you the push you need to try new recipes and explore the potential of different ingredients.

With the crowd-pleasing classic recipes, delicious dishes that you won't find anywhere else, and innovative recipes that will take your favorite avocado dishes to the next level, this book is sure to be a hit with any avo lover. Whether you are an experienced cook or a beginner, no matter your skill level, "Guac Your World" will be your go-to source for delicious and nutritious avocado recipes.

The recipes in "Guac Your World" are simple, creative, and fun to make. From ceviche and taco salads to guacamole cakes and avocado mousse, each recipe is unique and deliciously convenient. Whether you're looking for a quick meal or an impressive dish to serve at a party, there is something for you in this cookbook.

Overall, "Guac Your World: 100 Recipes for Avocado Lovers" is an invaluable resource for anyone who loves avocados or wants to experience all the flavor and nutrition the humble avocado can bring. The recipes are easy to follow and enjoyable to make, and the book's clear descriptions and tempting photographs will inspire you to create something delicious. Whether you are looking for a simple snack or a gourmet dinner, this cookbook is sure to bring you joy and satisfaction!

Printed in Great Britain
by Amazon